Six Steps to B⟨ Learning

This inspirational and reader-friendly guide offers school leaders six quick and achievable steps for transforming teaching and learning into a high-impact action plan. Author Karen A. Goeller shows how effective curriculum, instruction, and assessment work can help students overcome college, career, and life challenges. With its clear steps and concrete advice, this text will help school leaders in any district ignite passion for continuous school improvement and sustain a culture of ongoing and collaborative learning.

Topics include:

- crafting a purpose statement that will rally students, teachers, and families around an essential focus;
- using data to boost school improvement and student performance;
- streamlining curriculum and instruction;
- building meaningful relationships among students, teachers, and families;
- leveraging instructional strategies to improve student engagement; and
- energizing staff and students with networking strategies and transition activities.

Each chapter offers research tips, guides to action, numerous examples, reflection questions, immediate take-aways, and downloadable tools.

Karen A. Goeller is Deputy Superintendent for the Vigo County School Corporation in Indiana, and Adjunct Instructor of Educational Leadership at Indiana State University.

Other Eye On Education Books
Available from Routledge
(www.routledge.com/eyeoneducation)

Ten Steps for Genuine Leadership in Schools
David M. Fultz

**College for Every Student: A Practitioner's Guide to Building
College and Career Readiness**
Rick Dalton and Edward P. St. John

Leading Learning for ELL Students: Strategies for Success
Catherine Beck and Heidi Pace

Leadership in America's Best Urban Schools
Joseph F. Johnson, Jr., Cynthia L. Uline, and Lynne G. Perez

**The Power of Conversation: Transforming Principals into
Great Leaders**
Barbara Kohm

**First Aid for Teacher Burnout: How You Can Find Peace
and Success**
Jenny G. Rankin

**What Successful Principals Do! 199 Tips for Principals,
2nd Edition**
Franzy Fleck

**The Revitalized Tutoring Center: A Guide to Transforming
School Culture**
Jeremy Koselak and Brad Lyall

7 Ways to Transform the Lives of Wounded Students
Joe Hendershott

**School Leadership through the Seasons: A Guide to Staying Focused
and Getting Results All Year**
Ann T. Mausbach and Kimberly Morrison

**Distributed Leadership in Schools: A Practical Guide for Learning
and Improvement**
John A. DeFlaminis, Mustafa Abdul-Jabbar, and Eric Yoak

**The Leader's Guide to Working with Underperforming Teachers:
Overcoming Marginal Teaching and Getting Results**
Sally Zepeda

**Five Critical Leadership Practices: The Secret to
High-Performing Schools**
Ruth C. Ash and Pat H. Hodge

**Strategies for Developing and Supporting School Leaders:
Stepping Stones to Great Leadership**
Karen L. Sanzo

Six Steps to Boost Student Learning

A Leader's Guide

Karen A. Goeller

Routledge
Taylor & Francis Group

NEW YORK AND LONDON

First published 2018
by Routledge
711 Third Avenue, New York, NY 10017

and by Routledge
2 Park Square, Milton Park, Abingdon, Oxon, OX14 4RN

Routledge is an imprint of the Taylor & Francis Group, an informa business

Library of Congress Cataloging in Publication Data
A catalog record for this book has been requested

ISBN: 978-1-138-23979-1 (hbk)
ISBN: 978-1-138-23980-7 (pbk)
ISBN: 978-1-315-29493-3 (ebk)

Typeset in Optima
by Florence Production Ltd, Stoodleigh, Devon, UK

Visit the eResources: https://www.routledge.com/9781138239807

Contents

Contents

<#>

About the Author

Karen A. Goeller has over 30 years of education experience. She has a PhD in educational administration and an MA in English. She serves as deputy superintendent in a large Midwestern school district and is an adjunct instructor for graduate leadership education. She has taught English and journalism in public and private middle and high schools in Texas, Louisiana, Mississippi, Tennessee, and Indiana. She has also served as a dean of students, a middle and high school assistant principal, and district curriculum director. She has served on state educational technology and service learning committees. Karen was honored with a Wabash Valley Women of Influence Award, a North Central Association Outstanding Administrator Award, Phi Delta Kappa International Outstanding Dissertation Award, Junior Achievement Educator of the Year Award, and Educational Heritage Association Educator of the Year Award. Along with teachers and administrators in her district, she co-authored the *Instructional Unit Planning Manual* with Dr. Robert Marzano. Karen also received a leadership foundation grant to travel to schools in five urban cities to research higher levels of student achievement. She has published articles about the teenage brain in conjunction with a Harvard researcher and contributed an article for a state bicentennial book. She was honored with the 2017 Golden Quill Award for Excellence in Writing. Karen can be reached at karen.goeller@yahoo.com.

Preface

Why I Wrote This Book

Stakes are extremely high as students move through K-12 classrooms and schools along the complex and ever-evolving pathway toward success. How can we best prepare students for the critical thinking, creative problem solving, and twenty-first-century communication skills needed for higher education demands, rapidly expanding technology, and a globally competitive workforce? How can we best guide students to emerge from K-12, ready to persist as learners and to act as responsible and caring citizens?

School leaders are working feverishly in school improvement efforts to ensure that all students are moving toward higher goals. Most certainly, good teaching and learning matters in ensuring each student's future success. School leaders must be deeply intentional about aligning college, career, and life expectations with the good teaching and learning work that needs to take place in classrooms and schools.

Teaching and learning is the toughest and most visible part of the school leader's job. Like the definition of student success, the meaning of school success is also multi-faceted. The good news is that we DO have access to valid and reliable educational research. We DO know from researchers and practitioners about those teaching and learning practices that have proven effects and widespread applications. And, we DO know from school leaders about what works in various settings for certain students. School leaders are desperately seeking that "aha moment" when ease meets high-impact, and the right teaching and learning components come together in an all-in-one plan.

What You Will Find

This book offers school leaders six quick and achievable steps to transform teaching and learning into a lean plan, driving greater student outcomes and resulting in a better school culture. The book has four primary objectives:

- to empower principals and teachers to lead the Every Student Succeeds Act [ESSA] (2015) flexibly with useful, confidence-boosting steps;
- to provide evidence-based strategies that enable students to reach higher college, career, and life goals;
- to solve the very real needs of crazy-busy practitioners by streamlining teaching and learning big components into a high quality plan; and
- to ignite passion for continuous school improvement and sustain a culture of ongoing and collaborative learning.

Purpose and intentional design are essential to exceptional performance. Good teaching and learning involves prioritizing and streamlining the essential components. Innovation does not have to be bigger and more complex. Too many scattered and disjointed teaching and learning parts are more problematic for school leaders than not enough. Six field-proven and hyper-practical steps will translate purpose into action and yield big results.

Practitioner voices and professional connections are needed for school leaders to bring about a culture of sustained, continuous improvement. Growing student learning requires growing teacher learning. School leaders will take on new roles and build more robust relationships with others to bring about real change. Great leadership is shared leadership as educators learn and grow together.

What Is the Organization of This Book?

School leaders are always learners first. After a brief introduction, principals and teachers will find six high-impact components that will allow them to reimagine teaching and learning and accelerate student growth in classrooms and schools.

Step One: Focus on What Matters Most for Students

School leaders will begin with the basics of good teaching and learning. Crafting and communicating a teaching and learning purpose statement will rally students, teachers, and families around an essential focus. School leaders will then be armed with research and legislative guidance to set an aggressive equity agenda and ensure that all students have rich opportunities to learn. School leaders will assist students in developing growth mindsets and foster the grit and agency necessary to move them to deeper learning. School leaders will interact with clear descriptions of college and career targets and learn easy ways to communicate the critical information to families. When it comes to the big lesson of teaching and learning, principals and teachers must be visionary leaders, well versed and equipped to prepare students for what is headed their way.

Step Two: Lead Learning with Easy Data Use

A conceptualization model will assist school leaders in organizing the data work while moving students closer to college, career, and life goals. Data work will energize school improvement, professional development, classroom instruction, and student performance and growth. Principals and teachers will use their own collaborative data protocol to embed meaningful practices into the culture of the school. Teachers will become instructional leaders who drive student learning with real-time data use. Focusing on the process of growth will help students better understand their learning and make real gains. Interactive data activities will draw families into the school as active partners in their children's learning.

Step Three: Prioritize and Simplify Curriculum and Instruction

Step three brings the thunder in streamlining curriculum and instruction. School leaders will optimize the use of local curriculum, including standards, textbooks and supplementary materials, pacing guides, and unit and lesson plans. Quality classroom instruction includes simple instructional routines and evidence-based, engaging strategies. The higher college and career targets will become reachable for students as school leaders better align the needed reading and writing skills and abilities. School leaders will engage with effective and implementation-ready reading and writing practices to prepare students for higher education and the workplace. Downloadable tools will help school leaders immediately impact students' quality and quantity of reading and writing opportunities.

Step Four: Strengthen Learning with Relationship Building

Step four features school leaders who have the know-how and the passion to build intentional relationships among students, teachers, and families that bring about greater student outcomes. Building student capacity begins in quality classrooms as teachers strategically differentiate learning to meet the needs of all students. Principals and teachers also accelerate student capacity through design of classroom teams. Capacity building for principals and teachers involves embedded professional development using modeling and coaching and school improvement rounds. Engaging families in meaningful partnerships builds trusting relationships and more learning.

Step Five: Leverage Powerful Pieces to Accelerate Growth

Strategically adding BIG pieces to good teaching and learning will boost and energize the work of students, teachers, families, and school leaders themselves. Principals and teachers will give students rigorous speaking and learning opportunities and power up learning. Vocabulary achievement will increase through direct instruction, wide reading, and schoolwide vocabulary applications. School leaders will enhance achievement with active social studies instruction, using biographies and autobiographies, community learning, historical storytelling, service learning, and citizenship learning. Schoolwide literacy strategies will continue to stretch student learning. The grant writing process will spur on school leaders and grant writing teams to find creative solutions that support all students.

Step Six: Energize Staff and Students for the Next School Year

Principals and teachers must invest in their own leadership and learning, modeling a passion for continual inquiry about the latest teaching and learning research and emerging trends. Fresh, implementation-ready net-working strategies will engage leaders at the school, university, and state levels. Ideas are illustrated for supporting new teachers through mentoring, shadowing, staff development, and a teacher think tank. School leaders will inspire the best teachers by showcasing their skills, empowering them in new roles, and enabling them to lead professional conversations. Jump-starting the school year for students with proven transition activities will promote optimism and hope about college, career, and life success right from the start.

What Special Features Enhance This Book?

A beginning-of-chapter learning vignette invites readers into the real world of practicing school leaders, captured from my own teaching and administrative experiences in schools and districts in multiple states. An Essential Question sharpens the focus, stimulates thinking, and aids readers in making important connections among the upcoming strategies. Research Tips give school leaders the right information in bite-size chunks that are easy to communicate and share with others. Evidence-based strategies are presented that can be quickly and easily implemented in classrooms and schools. Stories from Educators Making a Difference Each Day give readers access points into the "hard work and heart" of principals and teachers in other school settings whose seemingly small actions bring consequential results. Guide to Action boxes weave practical applications strategically into each step. Numerous examples provide fresh ideas for easy replication. Reflection Questions provide more opportunities for readers to address what perplexes us. Leadership Take-Aways offer inspirational ways to apply the research and mobilize others to act. Downloadable Tools provide school leaders with ready resources for classroom and school use.

What Are Potential Uses of the Book?

Practicing and aspiring school leaders are always looking for ways to build teaching and learning cultures that boost student learning. This text takes a broader view of student and school success (beyond testing and accountability grades) yet also recognizes and relays the urgency in preparing students for the very real college and career challenges ahead.

This text challenges principals and teachers to grow new leadership and learning opportunities for students, teachers, and families. Building relationships and teams between and among adults and students enhances the school's capacity for powerful learning. Making fresh connections and forging innovative leadership roles in classrooms and schools create forward movement and more learning.

Principals and teachers are seeking the most useful school improvement resources. Each of the six steps can be used as a springboard for more comprehensive study and discussion. Reflection questions and leadership take-aways continue the dialogue for inquiry groups, team meetings, faculty retreats, and networking meetings. Even better, perhaps the questions and take-aways stimulate conversation and more creative ideas well into the evening at the local coffee shop.

School leaders deserve an easy read in their precious downtime. With its clear steps and concrete strategies, this text offers hyper-practical ideas to consider for implementation in a variety of settings. The stories may resonate with other school leaders and add a joyful moment in bringing back their own memories. Likewise, this text will serve as a guide to university leadership instructors about what is real in our honored profession.

Acknowledgments

My education colleagues, who are too numerous to name, have impacted this text the most. The journey to improve K-12 education continues with the vision and dedicated work of those in classrooms and schools every day who need to be acknowledged as the real heroes. I am the fortunate one who can tell their stories and mine, and hopefully make a contribution of lasting value to our profession.

I am deeply grateful to Routledge/Taylor & Francis Group, especially Heather Jarrow, whose editorial guidance was encouraging and spot-on from the start. She helped me seek out reviews of this manuscript early in the process, which were extremely beneficial. Likewise, I am grateful to Rebecca Collazo, Editorial Assistant, for her manuscript preparation guidance. Also, I thank Kinsey Norman for her graphics assistance.

I am grateful to my superintendent, Daniel Tanoos, and my district colleagues as we learn together every day. As I have worked and researched throughout several states, I am indebted to principals and teachers who have shared their authentic stories in the spirit of fellowship and more learning. My parents, Barbara and Jack Webster, and my husband's parents, Barbara and David Goeller, have also added joy and inspiration to my life.

I thank my husband, Michael Goeller, for his unconditional support. As I work to become a better educator, he always has the words to ground me in what is right. Finally, having two children of my own just complete college (Scott from business school and Kate from medical school) has made me acutely aware of the enormous challenges that families face and of the awesome responsibility that school leaders must acknowledge and act upon to prepare our K-12 students.

eResources

Keep an eye out for the eResources icon throughout this book, which indicates a resource is available online. Resources mentioned in this book can be downloaded, printed, used to copy/paste text, and/or manipulated to suit your individualized use. You can access these downloads by visiting the book product page on our website: www.routledge.com/products/ 9781138239807. Then click on the tab that reads "eResources" and select the file(s) you need. The file(s) will download directly to your computer.

Tools available online

- eResource A SAT and ACT Discussion Checklist
- eResource B Data Literacy Discussion Questions
- eResource C Schoolwide Reading Analysis Questions
- eResource D Schoolwide Writing Analysis Questions
- eResource E School Improvement Rounds Learning Log
- eResource F Major Speaking and Listening Opportunities Chart
- eResource G Grant Implementation Activities Chart
- eResource H Teaching and Learning Interview Questions
- eResource I Teacher Mentoring Conversation Starters
- eResource J Transition Goals and Strategies Skyrocket Student Success

Introduction

The annual back-to-school meeting is about to begin in the auditorium. Students, teachers, and families await opening remarks. What if . . . instead of explaining school rules or this year's fundraiser, school leaders stepped up and addressed the good teaching and learning components that matter most for all students? The large screen behind them would spotlight students fully engaged in academic talk and classroom teams. What if . . . principals and teachers shared their commitment to helping all students build growth mindsets and take ownership of their learning? What if . . . school leaders then challenged students to become effective, everyday data users, working toward their own ambitious goals? What if . . . principals and teachers conveyed specific ways that students would accelerate wide reading and increase their reading stamina? What if . . . school leaders praised the modeling and coaching and school improvement rounds that were spurring collective growth in good teaching? What if . . . school leaders previewed schoolwide service learning activities that would transform students into academic leaders and responsible citizens? And then, what if . . . school leaders closed by inviting families to join in vibrant and meaningful partnerships that would enhance learning for their children?

What if . . . school leaders advocated such clear and powerful steps that would push all students closer to their postsecondary and workforce goals? With principals and teachers serving as enthusiastic champions of teaching and learning, the auditorium atmosphere quickly swells with hope and possibilities. Good teaching and learning has begun. This simple guide will help school leaders prepare and stand ready for such an annual meeting.

Preview of the Book's Essential Content

Six Steps to Boost Student Learning: A Leader's Guide arms school leaders with clear and achievable steps to bring about quality teaching and learning and prepare K-12 students for the college, career, and life challenges ahead. Readers will interact with evidence, rich experiences, and practitioner voices as they think more deeply about accelerating meaningful outcomes for students. Each step begins with an overarching question to help school leaders conceptualize what is essential for good teaching and learning.

Step One: How Do School Leaders Focus on What Matters Most for Students?

How do school leaders even begin to create an environment that will enable all students to reach college, career, and life goals? School leaders who couple passion with a teaching and learning purpose are ready to seek out the rich learning opportunities that all students deserve. Advocating and acting for school fairness and building growth-oriented thinking across the school pushes the learning forward. With the right strategies, students become gritty and agency-ready for joining the global workforce. School leaders must translate the college and career expectations ahead into understandable language and create know-how for families to help their children.

Step Two: How Do School Leaders Use Data Strategically and Easily to Enhance the Quality of Teaching and Achieve Greater Student Outcomes?

Too much data can be overwhelming, and not knowing which data to collect and why can be even more frustrating. Using a clear model, school leaders can better conceptualize their data use and prioritize areas in which to act. Principals and teachers can develop their own collaborative data protocol and seize the right ingredients to move forward aggressively in school improvement efforts. School leaders will urge teachers to accept new leadership roles in collecting and studying plentiful classroom and school data. Even families will become passionate data users when they join their children in monitoring growth.

Step Three: How Do School Leaders Ensure the Highest Quality of Curriculum and Instruction?

Curriculum and instruction can become an unwieldy arena with too many disconnected parts. School leaders are often required to develop local curriculum, but what does that look like? Directing others will become easier with simple instructional routines and evidence-based, engaging strategies. Instead of looking with skepticism at the unbelievable expectations within the college and career targets, school leaders will thoughtfully align their similar components and move forward with ease. School leaders will recognize what higher levels of reading and writing instruction should look like in classrooms and gain confidence and new ideas for change.

Step Four: How Do School Leaders Build Capacity for Teaching and Learning among Students, Teachers, and Families?

Building capacity for greater learning involves intentional relationship building among students, teachers, and families. Differentiation strategies and team-building add energy to classrooms and boost student capacity. Modeling and coaching allow teachers themselves to design the learning that best helps them determine which teaching practices work for which students. Likewise, school improvement rounds give principals and teachers other chances to participate in inquiry around individual and schoolwide goals. Confidence about meeting students' needs expands as principals and teachers develop new leadership capacities. Purposeful school and family partnerships will result in stronger relationships and better learning.

Step Five: What Additional Pieces Can School Leaders Leverage to Accelerate Student Growth?

School leaders have many innovative, yet untapped BIG pieces to bring to the teaching and learning table. How many times do teachers really leverage the value of speaking and listening in improving student achievement? Immersing the school in irresistible vocabulary words and phrases powers up learning without costing the school a dime! Social studies instruction adds vibrancy and active engagement while building better citizens and stronger minds. Implementing higher levels of literacy standards across all content areas brings experimentation with different strategies for deeper learning. Grant writing fast-tracks growth and is an amazing lever for molding coalitions of support for students.

Step Six: How Can School Leaders Use the Summer Break to Design Powerful Activities that Jump-Start Learning for the Upcoming School Year?

Summer break is the time to invest in learning and prioritize those activities that will have the most impact for students in the upcoming year. School leaders who advance their own knowledge base can then lead important conversations about child development, direct curriculum, instruction, and assessment, and contribute to decisions about high-yield practices. Networking with colleagues brings fresh associations and creative ideas. Having a comprehensive plan in place for new teachers relieves anxiety and moves the learning forward. And, nurturing the top performers brings unlimited chances for renewal and professional satisfaction. Powerful student transition activities will ready new and incoming students for a phenomenal school year.

ESSA Offers Frameworks and Fresh Possibilities

The Every Student Succeeds Act [ESSA] (2015) brings legislative guidance about topics that matter most to students and schools. ESSA's elements of fairness, opportunities to learn, multiple assessment measures, monitoring of student growth, and principal and teacher development align seamlessly with good teaching and learning. School leaders must grab ESSA's critical elements to frame school improvement efforts and drive greater teaching and learning.

ESSA (2015) ushers in optimism about leadership and learning possibilities at the school and district levels. Principals, teachers, students, and families can remix roles and strengthen relationships that result in more learning. Yes, ESSA requires testing on challenging standards, demands accountability for progress, and has consequences for low-performing schools (2015). However, the federal law also specifically recognizes practitioner expertise and experience in directing evidence-based practices that help students meet these challenges. At the same time, ESSA adds to the national conversation about a fair definition of school quality and student success and confirms other indicators, such as student and teacher engagement (2015). The time is ripe for school leaders to think in new ways about adding intensity and enthusiasm to leadership and learning. ESSA favors state and local leaders as the ones to step up with the right people, the right structures, the right data, and the right processes to take on the challenges ahead (2015). School leaders have chances to get it right!

Professional Standards Build Stronger Leaders

Building stronger school leaders results in stronger students with stronger minds! As school leaders engage in the good teaching and learning practices within this text, their work will be supported by the Professional Standards for Educational Leaders 2015 (National Policy Board for Educational Administration). Steps in this book are well aligned with professional standards about equity, curriculum, instruction, assessment, professional community, engagement of students and teachers, and school improvement. The professional standards have a renewed focus on student learning, specifically to prepare all students for twenty-first-century challenges. This book will provide a context for rich conversations around applications of the respected national standards.

A Word of Encouragement

School leaders have ESSA's (2015) critical elements along with strong professional standards as important foundations for their good teaching and learning work. With these frameworks in hand, school leaders can now add evidence, proven experiences, and rich practitioner voices. With a better understanding of the challenges ahead and with colleagues who want to grow learning along with students, school leaders are ready to make the journey. As we move forward with these six promising and proven steps, we will improve leadership, build a better school culture, and grow greater student outcomes.

References

Every Student Succeeds Act, Public Law 114–95, December 10, 2015; 129 Stat. 1802 (2015).

National Policy Board for Educational Administration. (2015). Professional Standards for Educational Leaders 2015. Reston, VA: Author.

Focus on What Matters Most for Students

Simple Strategies

- ◼ **Use Purpose to Motivate**
- ◼ **Ensure Equity and Opportunities to Learn**
- ◼ **Advocate for Growth Mindsets**
- ◼ **Push for Grit and Agency**
- ◼ **Communicate College and Career Targets**
- ◼ **Eliminate the Distractors**

I vividly recall first impressions of teaching and learning in several schools. One thing was certain on that very first day . . . either school leaders had a clear plan for teaching and learning or they did not. The majority of school leaders handed us duty rosters and left us to scurry up and down hallways for curriculum guides. One school, however, stands out where the principal and teachers placed good teaching and learning front and center. New teachers were treated to a spirited panel where students connected their college and career aspirations with the school's curricular offerings. Students bantered fondly about challenging each other in Socratic seminars, trying new roles in the school musical, and manipulating the wrong variables in science experiments. Students had contagious, can-do attitudes and were in charge of their own learning. School leaders then shared the teaching and learning purpose statement, which reinforced the school's strong commitment to preparing students for postsecondary and workplace success. As a new teacher, I quickly gained confidence in the principal and teachers who zeroed in on what mattered most for students. These school leaders knew where their students were headed and were effective in rallying others to help students accomplish their goals.

ESSENTIAL QUESTION

HOW DO SCHOOL LEADERS FOCUS ON WHAT MATTERS MOST FOR STUDENTS?

At the beginning of each school year, principals and teachers must grab the one-time window of opportunity to kick off the school's teaching and learning plan. No other Chief Executive Officer in business, industry, or nonprofit sectors has a fresh start every year, and this is the time to place attention where it matters most for students. Principals and teachers are very good at starting with critical background knowledge to enable students to spring forward in their learning. However, when it comes to planning for the BIG schoolwide lesson of teaching and learning, we often short-change everyone . . . ourselves, teachers, families, and, most of all, students, when we do not build our own knowledge base, focus our attention, and ready ourselves to connect with students' college, career, and life goals.

RESEARCH TIP

Clear Direction Leads to Academic Gains

Marzano, Waters, and McNulty (2005) examined 69 studies in a meta-analysis to learn more about behaviors of principal leadership. Findings reveal an important correlation of the principal's behavior of "focus" with student academic achievement (p. 42). When the principal sets clear goals and directs the school's attention to these goals, students are more likely to make greater academic achievement (p. 42).

2

Warren Buffett and Bill Gates, highly successful leaders in their respective financial and technological fields, both comment about the importance of having focus in achieving their successes in life (Schroeder, 2009, p. 623). Schroeder describes other leaders who have this type of focus, pointing to their discipline, commitment, and intensity needed to achieve excellence (2009, p. 624). Boldly and intentionally, school leaders, too, must go out front early in the year with a laser focus on student development and success.

Use Purpose to Motivate

Student Outcomes

School leaders who focus on what matters most for students begin with purpose. Too often, principals and teachers work day after day, putting in dreadfully long hours, without taking time to stop and re-focus on the reasons behind good teaching and learning. It is critical to help students derive meaning from the experiences they have in school and think more clearly about how these experiences will improve their options for future education and employment. School leaders must guide students, teachers, and families to re-assess the *why* of school and gain a clearer perspective of pathways to better student outcomes.

What it means for students to find success after the K-12 experience is still evolving. Just as business leaders must continuously predict where markets and global economies are heading and communicate goals and targets to others, school leaders must stand ready to do the same. Students, teachers, and families need school leaders who deeply understand child development yet are equally well prepared to push students closer to college, career, and life goals. School leaders must continuously scan the horizon, update their own knowledge about increasing expectations, and relentlessly communicate education and workforce readiness priorities to students and families.

STORIES FROM EDUCATORS MAKING A DIFFERENCE EACH DAY

Focusing on student outcomes in a faculty meeting was especially insightful and enjoyable for me. School leaders provided our small groups with chart paper displaying stick figures with protruding arms and legs. The groups were asked to name the newly graduated K-12 stick figures and select their career goals. My group's figure was Carter with a career goal of becoming a physical therapist. We then reflected: When this student leaves our school, what does the student need to know and be able to do? On our chart paper, we surrounded our graduates with drawings of skills and abilities, transforming the figures into future employees, well-prepared for twenty-first century success in the global economy. Would Carter need advanced geometry skills? Would Carter need sophisticated reasoning skills? In our group, a healthy debate ensued about the multitude and range of cognitive and noncognitive abilities that Carter needed to reach his career goal. As teachers shared their artwork, conversations flowed about ways to bolster the needed abilities. Throughout the year, school leaders brought the graduates back out, and we continued the thoughtful conversations, promoting collective responsibility for equipping students for a changing world.

Purpose Statements

School leaders must guide others in crafting purpose statements for teaching and learning. As part of continuous improvement, schools have likely created overall vision and mission statements that address students' academic, social, emotional, and physical development. To keep an unmistakable focus on students and the college and career challenges ahead, principals and teachers will also need to extract from all continuous improvement efforts a clear teaching and learning purpose statement.

Examples of Teaching and Learning Purpose Statements

- Our teaching and learning will prepare students to be successful in college, careers, and life.
- Our students will be ready for college and career success in an evolving global economy.
- Our teaching and learning will enable all students to seek ambitious career and life goals.
- Our school will prepare all students to find success in the twenty-first-century workplace.
- All students will have robust learning opportunities to meet post-secondary and workplace goals.
- Students will be inspired and ready to seek greater challenges in future education and careers.
- Our students will develop intellectual abilities to the fullest to prepare for future goals.

RESEARCH TIP

Focusing on *Why* Motivates Others to Act

Pink (2009) examines four decades of research and points to purpose as needed for true motivation. Principals and teachers should help students see the larger picture of their learning. Students need to understand why they are learning certain information and how it is relevant to them (p. 179). To further explain motivation, Pink states that when people have a similar purpose, the group will be more likely to perform excellent work (p. 169).

With a teaching and learning purpose statement in hand, school leaders can then work intensely and in disciplined ways with students, teachers, and families toward that purpose. When principals and teachers embrace the *why* for students, purpose becomes the driver for making continuous improvements in teaching and learning. The teaching and learning purpose statement focuses the daily work of students and molds continuous learning within the school culture. Principals, teachers, students, and families are more motivated to work toward excellence when they have a similar purpose of improved student outcomes. Understanding the larger picture gives direction and relevance to the teaching and learning work.

School leaders can highlight the teaching and learning purpose statement in a wide variety of ways.

Ready Channels to Communicate the Teaching and Learning Purpose Statement

Report cards	Faculty agendas
Newsletters	School lunch menus
Classroom websites	School t-shirts
Learning management platform	Parent letters
Hallway banners	Student work folders
Social media blasts	Student handbooks

GUIDE TO ACTION

The Ball, a short parable, assists school leaders in conveying the significance of a teaching and learning purpose statement (Whitaker, 2010). Are we prioritizing our students' future goals? Asking various stakeholders to read playful parts aloud will generate laughter and enjoyment yet reinforce the larger purpose of why students are attending school.

Ensure Equity and Opportunities to Learn

Imagine a school where all students arrive with the newest digital devices in hand. Imagine a school where students are re-energized from a good night's sleep. Imagine a school where students have homes with bright lights and comfortable places to read. Imagine a school where a majority of students do not move throughout the year. Imagine a school where students discover bugs, trees, and flowers on weekends. Imagine a school where families debate international events at dinner.

Learning Gaps

Nowhere are gaps in student learning more noticeable than on the school's doorstep. Students arrive from various backgrounds with an incredibly wide range of academic and social experiences. Yet, all of these students want and need to leave K-12 schools prepared for success in the competitive global workforce. Right from the start, school leaders must advance rich and equitable learning opportunities.

STORIES FROM EDUCATORS MAKING A DIFFERENCE EACH DAY

In a large urban high school, our principal constantly walked the hallways to ensure that all students were engaged in learning. He was a firm believer that all students could learn when given equal chances. At an early faculty meeting, he asked us to write down a student's name who was a low performer, highly unmotivated, and perhaps the student we liked the least. Although there was a brief hush in the room, we were all able to quickly list a student. Then, he told us to keep that name private and begin to treat that student as if he were our top performer. Our principal said that we should adjust our attitudes toward this student and challenge him with our best teaching. It would be difficult, but we needed to find the ways ourselves. I later found myself smiling when this student arrived. When he put his head down in the middle of class, instead of getting frustrated, I urged him to join the group when he felt better. When I asked higher level questions, I prodded him enthusiastically to speculate and make predictions. I wrote more motivational phrases on his essays. Without a doubt, this pointed and humbling activity caused me to adopt more fair instructional practices.

A very real gap exists in students' learning opportunities. Many students have access to rich and diverse learning resources and experiences during and outside of school while others are denied the same chances. America's public schools should be the foundation of our democracy, yet the Equity and Excellence Commission asserts that the educational system is not fully serving all children (U.S. Department of Education, 2013, p. 12). School leaders must look for ways to reduce excellence and equity disparities to ensure that each child is successful and to guarantee that America can compete in the global economy. All students need opportunities to learn college- and career-ready standards and twenty-first-century skills like critical thinking, problem-solving, and communication (pp. 12–15). The Commission contends that students are denied access to high quality instruction when they are not taught core curriculum, given work that is low in academic rigor, and not provided with catch-up work or homework (2013, p. 27).

Equity and excellence do matter to every student. School leaders must confront the issue of fairness by leading discussions about student access to quality teaching and learning opportunities. School leaders must design school improvement work around equity and excellence goals. If students are not presented with optimal circumstances in which to master core curriculum during their K-12 education, they are unfairly denied chances that will narrow future education and employment choices.

RESEARCH TIP

Students Must Have Chances to Learn Content and Skills

All children must have chances to master important curriculum. Marzano, Warrick, and Simms (2014) include opportunity to learn within their high reliability schools framework. The researchers emphasize the need for students to have a "guaranteed and viable curriculum" that includes content with course and grade specifications as well as enough time for instruction of this content (2014, pp. 69–70).

Equity-Focused Improvement

The Every Student Succeeds Act [ESSA], (2015) promotes equity in learning in its guidance to states and schools.

Examples of ESSA's Elements of Equity

- Assessments are required in grades 3–8 and once in high school on challenging state academic standards in English/language arts, math, and science to enable students, teachers, and families to track each student's progress year by year.
- Assessment data indicate three levels of achievement, making clear which students are making growth and which students need more chances to learn in core curriculum.
- Assessment data are used to identify need for greater academic support for subgroups (poverty, special education, racial and ethnic, and English learners).
- Schools must set long-term goals and measurements of interim progress toward meeting those goals to ensure learning for all students and for each subgroup of students.
- Schools in the lowest-performing 5 percent of all schools and high schools failing to graduate one third or more of students will be identified for improvement.
- If improvement is needed, schools must develop comprehensive plans that support all students and identify resource inequities.

(ESSA, 2015)

Principals and teachers should leverage ESSA's focus on equity to drive school improvement (2015). To illustrate, ESSA requires all students to make growth on challenging state academic standards (2015). As part of continuous school improvement, principals, teachers, and families should regularly monitor student progress and benchmark interim growth. As another example, ESSA has the expectation that the lowest-performing students will be identified for additional support (2015). School leaders and grade level teacher teams can develop comprehensive individual learning plans to allocate high quality resources to low-performing students.

School leaders should advance equity as they work to improve practices within and outside of school.

School Improvement Checklist about Equity

☐ Do all students have access to core academic content, including rigorous standards?

☐ Do we regularly share performance and growth data about all students and student subgroups?

☐ Do we set schoolwide and classroom goals to address deficiencies for student subgroups?

☐ Do we schedule ongoing equity conversations and talk openly about disparities?

☐ Do we use effective strategies to engage all learners from bell-to-bell?

☐ Do we prioritize professional development that helps us create equitable classrooms?

☐ Do we provide catch-up work or homework to extend learning?

☐ Do we try to remove barriers, such as transportation, that impact program participation?

☐ Do we monitor the availability and effectiveness of our extended day programs?

RESEARCH TIP

All Students Need Access to the Best Resources

Darling-Hammond (2010) finds that children in the most affluent communities have the greatest resources while children in poor communities, especially in high-minority areas, have the fewest resources. Darling-Hammond shares evidence that high performing schools around the world find the best teachers and leaders, provide professional development to ensure teachers are well-prepared, and provide the highest quality of standards and twenty-first-century teaching and learning (2010, p. 26).

☐ Do we push ourselves to find the range of resources that students need?

☐ Do we assist all families in accessing vital information about their children's progress?

Extended Learning Opportunities

School leaders must enlist students as partners in ongoing equity conversations. How can the school improve in ensuring fairness and access to learning opportunities? Selecting students at random for focus groups ensures valid and reliable feedback. Beginning with the teaching and learning purpose statement, school leaders can ask students to describe the kinds of instructional activities taking place within the school and outside the school day. Then, principals and teachers can analyze responses as to quality and quantity of instructional activities and levels of student engagement. Is our teaching and learning resulting in desired outcomes for all students? By digging deeper into reasons for disparities in identified areas, principals and teachers can strengthen and expand learning activities.

RESEARCH TIP

Underserved Students Need More Quality Learning Opportunities

Low-income students need chances to engage in deeper learning both during the day and outside of schools (Noguera, Darling-Hammond, & Friedlaender, 2015, p. 2). Students of color and students in poverty must have access to rigorous curriculum if they are going to be prepared for college and careers (p. 4).

School leaders must intervene to ensure all students have access to robust learning opportunities. How can the school offer a greater quantity and more quality learning opportunities to underserved students? How can school leaders offer underserved students chances to extend learning like their more advantaged peers? School leaders should challenge teachers and families to investigate creative possibilities that extend learning.

Examples of Extended Learning Opportunities

Before/after school programs

Individual/small group tutoring

Enrichment clubs

Study groups

Saturday seminars

Self-paced modules

Visits to museums and libraries

Internships

Independent projects

School leaders should seek out higher education and local community organizations that offer students a broad array of learning opportunities. Many local providers have high quality, no-cost programs and would welcome school partnerships to generate enrollment during out-of-school time. Putting up flyers in hallways is not the same as visiting and working in tandem with providers to help individual students enroll. Working closely with local partners to align their programming opportunities with core content areas will avail students of deeper learning. Principals and teachers should monitor student participation and follow-up with providers to track progress and encourage persistence.

STORIES FROM EDUCATORS MAKING A DIFFERENCE EACH DAY

Reading a biography of a successful leader like Condoleezza Rice in a faculty or family study group raises awareness of potential student learning opportunities. Looking at real people and their pathways to success can inspire others to act. Rice's family valued academic and artistic development and exposed her to foreign languages, the piano, athletics, and classical books during the K-12 years (Felix, 2002). Her parents and teachers worked together to structure learning experiences in incremental steps that enabled Rice to cultivate academic, musical, and athletic talents. Making connections between home and school learning enabled Rice to achieve greater outcomes. Rice developed self-discipline and a passion for learning that translated into a lifelong study of international relations and the Soviet Union (2002, pp. 93–99).

Advocate for Growth Mindsets

How exciting it would be if all students stepped off buses each morning with bright eyes, hopeful attitudes, and self-confidence about learning! We want all students to believe they are capable of increasing their learning as they work toward challenging goals. We want students to enter the school each day ready to navigate their own paths toward greater learning.

RESEARCH TIP

Growth Mindsets Cultivate Stamina and More Learning

Dweck (2006) documents the impact of mindsets on student achievement. Students with fixed mindsets believe their achievement is limited which results in poor learning choices (p. 67). However, students with growth mindsets have unlimited learning strategies and do not quit trying (p. 59). Dweck (2006) conveys that students can reach high standards, and she urges teachers, parents, and coaches to motivate students using growth mindsets, teaching students to give maximum efforts and value mistakes (p. 212).

Growth-Oriented Thinking

With research and legislative guidance in hand, school leaders have new roles in guiding students to adopt more optimistic attitudes about learning. Students with fixed mindsets are at a clear disadvantage and need to learn why and how to cultivate a more developmental view of intelligence. With a fixed mindset about intelligence, students believe that their capabilities are predetermined and say things, such as, "I cannot get formulas. I have always been dumb at chemistry." These students become pessimistic, quit working, and give up.

Instead, adults in students' lives must advocate that all students can grow intelligence through efforts. Choosing words carefully reinforces efforts in learning. For example, principals and teachers should praise a student's self-motivation and strategy use with encouragement like, "You tried several problem solving methods, and look, this one works!" When teachers reinforce growth mindsets through words and actions, classrooms become safe places where students encounter setbacks yet know that their efforts are positive in helping them improve.

RESEARCH TIP

Growth Mindsets Better Predict Achievement than Income

Claro and Paunesku (2014) show the inequality of mindset distributions, with low income students being more likely to have fixed mindsets (p. B-4). Researchers found that 10th graders at every family income level with growth mindsets had higher levels of academic performance. Mindset was a better predictor of test scores than family income (p. B-4).

School leaders can use the following checklist to help teachers and families think more intentionally about language and actions that nurture growth mindsets.

Quick Check: Do You Promote Growth Mindsets?

☐ Do you emphasize that intelligence and talents can be developed through effort?

☐ Do you praise students who seek out and experiment with different strategies?

☐ Do you allow students to see you try new skills as a learner?

☐ Do you ask questions that illustrate your curiosity?

☐ Do you try innovative approaches in the classroom and share excitement of learning?

☐ Do you help students view mistakes as beneficial learning experiences?

☐ Do you bring objects from home to spark different kinds of learning?

- [ ] Do you share examples of your accomplishments and how they were linked to your efforts?
- [ ] Do you share examples of your failures and dissect what strategies did not work?
- [ ] Do you provide specific feedback on tasks so that students can make modifications and grow learning?
- [ ] Do you talk regularly about the words *efforts* and *improvement?*

Growth-Focused Classrooms

Principals and teachers must be relentless leaders who advance growth-oriented classrooms. If students are to be successful on increasingly difficult challenges, principals and teachers must be intentional in showing students that they can grow their intelligence. Teachers should embed explicit ways into daily instruction that students can see the value and the results of their efforts in their learning.

Classroom Practices that Power up Student Efforts

Demonstrate Learning with Standards—Teachers introduce lessons with standards that emphasize the process of learning. For example, science standards require students to build mastery over time through exploring, studying, and investigating.

Analyze Strategies—Students annotate strategies as they complete various work tasks. Students note which strategies are more effective in their learning than others. And, by breaking down the work tasks, students see more clearly the efforts needed to produce quality products.

Send Consistent Effort Messages—Teachers reflect upon ways that they acknowledge student achievement. How can we better recognize practice, multiple attempts, and efforts of learning as opposed to just rewarding outcomes? When students see that efforts matter, they adjust their thinking about how to develop intelligence.

Revise Projects—Students are given opportunities to rework projects for improved grades. By revising their work, students can better visualize their own developmental paths of learning.

Collaborate with Peers—Collaborative group work exposes students to growth-minded peers. Students gain understanding about growing learning when they hear how peers approach learning and make incremental improvements.

Ask Questions—Students learn that asking questions does not mean that you do not know; instead, it means you want to know more. Students are praised for asking good questions that stretch thinking as opposed to simply being recognized for giving correct answers.

STORIES FROM EDUCATORS MAKING A DIFFERENCE EACH DAY

While running errands one Saturday morning, I encountered a former middle school algebra teacher. He looked exactly the same, and, yes, he recognized me, too. Memories overwhelmed me . . . not thoughts about grades or tests, but lucid recollections about PROBLEM 25. As a class, we talked through algebra problems together, postulating about why this or that multi-step solution was better. Fascinated with math himself, this teacher praised efforts in trying alternate strategies and valued our mistakes along the way. "Keep trying" was the Room 210 way. Throughout the year, he challenged all of us with PROBLEM 25, the last one in each chapter. Students would hurry to school to grapple with the problem together. This teacher believed that we all could work PROBLEM 25, and his belief in our abilities led us to develop confidence and build stronger minds.

Push for Grit and Agency

How many students come to mind who are very bright as measured by standardized tests but who do not perform well or persist in class activities? And, how many of these students make it through high school but later come back and acknowledge defeat in demanding college coursework? However, are there other students who come to mind who did not score well on standardized tests but who were able to confront adversity and go on to achieve college, career, and life goals? How do school leaders guide students to sustain efforts amid challenges and persist in their learning?

RESEARCH TIP

Noncognitive Factors Shape Definition of Student Success

Farrington et al. (2012) acknowledge the significance of noncognitive factors in determining student grades and college success. Students who participate in class, study, complete challenging work, and persist with tasks get higher grades (p. 73). Student grades show evidence of behaviors, attitudes, and strategies and better predict outcomes than standardized tests (p. 3).

Research confirms that students who engage in class work and persist amidst challenges earn better grades (Farrington et al., 2012). Like research studies, educational conversations and legislative debates are ongoing about the need for a more balanced definition of student and school success. Measuring student or school success by standardized test scores only does not provide a full or accurate picture about students' capabilities. How are students who perform poorly on state achievement tests able to make top grades in their coursework? What noncognitive factors push students to greater learning during their K-12 experiences? And, which of the noncognitive factors will then propel students to find greater success in college, career, and life pursuits? Besides cognitive skills, what other abilities must students possess to engage in the higher level thinking, problem solving, innovation, and communication skills demanded by the globally competitive workplace?

Grit

School leaders must go out front and advance a broader view in defining and in demonstrating student learning. Yes, improving student performance and growth involves accelerating content knowledge and skills, but it also includes other powerful learning factors. Principals and teachers must boost students' development of important noncognitive factors, such as grit, that can drive greater student achievement.

RESEARCH TIP

Grit Leads to Student Success

Duckworth, Peterson, Matthews, and Kelly (2007) studied achievements of prominent leaders and found that their successes depended both on talent and grit (p. 1100). Individuals with grit work persistently toward goals, even amidst adversity. Teachers should guide students to work with intensity and with stamina (p. 1100). In describing grit, Duckworth shares that highly successful individuals have both passion and perseverance (2016, p. 8). Duckworth explains that many people quit too early while gritty people overcome obstacles and keep going (2016, p. 50).

How do principals and teachers create environments where students want to keep working, even amid setbacks? How can teachers support students yet give them opportunities to struggle? Principals and teachers should design classroom instruction that gives students opportunities to build tenacity and stamina. For instance, teachers can coach students to set challenging goals and help them self-monitor progress toward the goals. As students encounter roadblocks, teachers can encourage students to adopt different strategies and persist in learning.

How can principals and teachers act and model behaviors that move students to develop grit?

Easy Ways to Help Students Develop Grit

- Praise students who work harder and take risks.
- Be a gritty leader and struggle alongside students in challenging projects.
- Recognize stamina by displaying student work in draft or practice stages.
- Highlight individuals who pushed beyond limits and accomplished greatness.

- Write a personal goal to recognize resilience in as many students as possible.

- Invite teachers to share ways they support students in overcoming setbacks.

- Use social media to communicate students' hard work and accomplishments to families.

- Invite the news media to interview students who have overcome obstacles.

- Chart the hours of practice by well-known musicians and athletes.

- Help students find ways to sustain hobbies and special interests.

- Present the school leader's grit award throughout the year.

Agency

Like grit, agency is a powerful noncognitive factor that influences student success in school and beyond. Why are some students self-motivated and empowered to take the next step while others remain passive in their learning? To support students as they reach for higher goals, school leaders must guide students in taking ownership of their learning. Students who become active and self-directed learners during the K-12 experience will have much more to offer the global workforce. To be successful in the many challenges ahead, students need to be able to think deeply and then act upon their learning.

RESEARCH TIP

Success Includes Noncognitive Factors Like Agency

Nagaoka et al. (2015) acknowledge agency as a major factor in young adult success (p. 2). To be prepared for successful futures, students must be able to seek and meet their own goals and then have the agency and abilities to engage as citizens in the world (2015, pp.1–2).

Classrooms and schools should be places where students make choices and decisions about their learning. Students become more self-directed in learning when they understand the relevance of school work to their project goals and outcomes. Teachers should design independent and small group performance tasks where students have autonomy during all stages of the learning process. School leaders should also ensure that students have opportunities across the school to participate in larger-scale projects that allow them to take responsibility for project outcomes.

Principals and teachers can easily embed chances for students to engage in agency-building activities within classrooms and across the school.

Simple Ways to Empower Students with Agency

Blended learning allows students to practice agency in an online environment, acting responsibly in learning spaces. When students have all-the-time access to new content and resources, they have chances to create, produce, and grow as independent learners. Teachers serve as coaches as students drive individual learning.

Project-based learning allows students to act in achieving the goals that they desire. Students assess their knowledge and available resources and then decide which steps are needed to move forward. Students gain self-discipline and experience commitment as they monitor their own goals throughout project creation.

Collages open up wider possibilities for self-expression and deeper learning. Students use reasoning skills and make decisions in collage creation. As students describe abstract concepts using various hands-on materials, they engage in self-discovery. Digital renditions give additional options for producing and owning work.

Authentic learning exposes students to real issues and new passions in the larger community. As students build knowledge and skills around tasks that have relevance to their own lives, they not only accelerate academic skills but they learn to advocate for themselves and others.

Portfolio assessments enable students to chronicle intellectual progress over time and think more deeply about strengths and weaknesses in their work. Justifying their progress to others encourages students to visualize self-growth and take responsibility for their learning. As students independently complete their work, rubrics give clear direction and promote agency.

Simple Questions for a Portfolio Assessment Rubric

- Did I write an overall goal for my portfolio assessment project?
- Did I make a timeline for completion of the required tasks?
- Did I create an outline of what I wanted to include in my portfolio?
- Did I follow directions about the variety and types of required artifacts?
- Did I choose outstanding assignments or work tasks for my portfolio?
- Did I seek feedback to improve the quality of my portfolio?
- Did I complete the reflections necessary for my portfolio?

Academic fairs encourage students to tap natural curiosity and make choices about interests to pursue outside the classroom. To build agency, teachers can set progress benchmarks to ensure students stay on track as they prepare individual and group competition products. Accepting responsibility to display and speak about their work to others enhances academic and social competencies.

RESEARCH TIP

Technology Fosters Agency in Learning

Technology tools enable students to develop greater ownership in their learning. The National Education Technology Plan (U.S. Department of Education, Office of Educational Technology, 2016) advocates for students to become innovative and productive technology users in areas such as coding, media production, design, interaction with experts, and collaboration with peers (p. 18). Students also foster agency by actively using immersive simulations and making global connections (p. 18).

Technology use opens up more avenues for students to develop agency. Students can set their own goals, seek out experts, and collaborate with peers across the globe. Different types of active learning and worldwide networking provide chances for students to participate fully and become more in control of their learning.

Although many questions remain unanswered about the interplay of factors that determine student success, research clearly points to the need for school leaders to embrace noncognitive factors in a more inclusive definition of student achievement. Bolstering teaching and learning with rich noncognitive factors like grit and agency will move students closer to life goals.

Communicate College and Career Targets

Although the definition of student success is complex and ever-evolving, school leaders must share with students, teachers, and families more about what we do know. High school leaders, especially, want to avoid conversations with students and families who experience frustration at the end of K-12 schooling. If only someone had told me . . . If I had only known more about . . . graduation requirements, the graduation exam, college admissions criteria, career pathways, and dual credit courses . . . I would have worked harder . . . I would have done things so much differently.

It's too late now . . . is not part of a discussion that school leaders want to have with students and families. Instead, school leaders must be proactive in preventing those way too common and unfortunate scenarios. Information is powerful, and school leaders must add knowledge building and communication sharing about college and career targets to the school's teaching and learning plan.

Beginning in elementary and extending through high school, school leaders need to explain the make-up of college and career readiness. What academic components contribute to the definition of being college and career ready? School leaders must first understand the targets themselves. Then, school leaders must communicate college and career information regularly to students and families in clear and user-friendly ways.

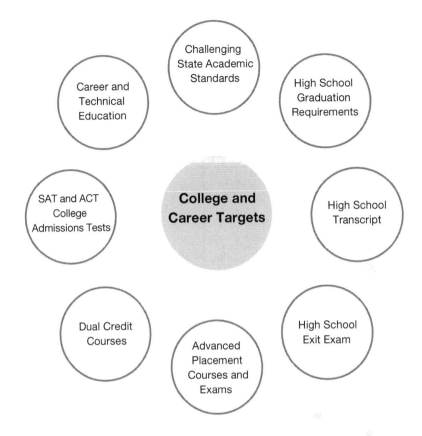

Figure 1.1 College and Career Targets

Challenging State Academic Standards

ESSA (2015) requires states to adopt challenging academic standards in mathematics, reading or language arts, and science. Common standards determine learning goals for what K-12 students should know and be able to do at the end of each grade. ESSA requires standards to align with entrance requirements for credit-bearing coursework in the State's system of public higher education and with relevant State career and technical education standards (2015).

To date, 42 states, and the District of Columbia, have adopted the Common Core State Standards (CCSS) for K-12 English/language arts and mathematics. Due to a partnership between the National Governors Association and the Council of Chief State School Officers, the CCSS have brought higher expectations to learning across the majority of states and have more consistently defined what knowledge and skills students need to succeed after high school (NGA & CCSSO, 2010).

> ### GUIDE TO ACTION
>
> School leaders should showcase the higher standards in ready venues. For instance, when students display projects at school events, such as academic fairs, school leaders should ask students to explain specific standards that have guided their learning. Giving incremental bites about rigorous standards throughout the year will help students and families grasp the big picture ahead.

High School Graduation Requirements

What it takes to earn a diploma cannot be overemphasized to students and families. Each state has different course requirements, and then local school boards may add other courses. Levels of diplomas, from general to technical to honors, are available to students. School leaders must reinforce that earning a diploma is based on a progression of learning. Education at the elementary and middle levels provides the foundation for high school graduation.

High School Transcript

College officials look first at the high school transcript when making admissions decisions, noting grades and courses taken, paying close attention to course difficulty and grade trends during high school (The College Board, 2015, p. 26). College admissions officers want to admit students who have taken a broad range of challenging classes and performed well in them. A pattern of improved grades from the freshman to senior year shows potential for greater learning.

Grades are signs of competencies not found on standardized tests. High grades reflect noncognitive factors, like grit and agency, that will lead students to greater success after high school.

High School Exit Exam

After attending school regularly and earning necessary credits, families assume their children will graduate with a diploma. However, in 19 states, beyond attendance and credit rules, exit exams or metrics will determine whether students receive high school diplomas (Zinth, 2016).

Exit exams are aligned to challenging state academic standards. School leaders must share blueprints of exam contents with students and families throughout the K-12 years.

STORIES FROM EDUCATORS MAKING A DIFFERENCE EACH DAY

Many families simply need direction in helping their children with college and career planning. And, if schools do not take the lead, the planning does not happen. As an example . . . my father was an extremely bright man who did not obtain a college degree. On one of our long walks, my father quietly shared the reason. Growing up, he lived above a tavern with parents who worked extremely hard to provide for the family, but they had no time to think about their children's long-term goals. They had no idea about preparations needed for their children to attend college, nor did they possess the know-how of seeking assistance to guide their children. My father talked about elementary teachers who were inspiring and supportive, but then said in middle and high school he was given little guidance about why or how to seek further education. After my father passed away, that memory has been a poignant one, and I have continually challenged myself to help students access higher education.

Advanced Placement Courses and Exams

The College Board's Advanced Placement (AP) program allows students to self-select high school courses and earn credit and/or advanced standing in colleges and universities (2017). Enrolling in college-level courses while in high school allows students to challenge themselves in a safer environment. The College Board offers over 35 courses in the arts, English, history and social sciences, math and computer science, sciences, and world languages and cultures (2017). Almost all U.S. colleges and universities award credit and placement for qualifying exam scores (The College Board, 2017).

AP courses on transcripts are well-known marks of achievement. The College Board ensures common syllabi, teacher training, and course audit system to monitor quality across high schools. At the end of each course, students take exams to earn college credit and/or placement in college courses. The College Board publishes criteria about colleges and their AP credit policies that school leaders can display so that students and families can see how credits are awarded by different institutions (The College Board, 2017).

With annual costs for undergraduate tuition, fees, room, and board estimated at $15,640.00 at public institutions in 2013–14 (U.S. Department of Education, National Center for Education Statistics, 2016), the prospect of free credits prior to entering college is appealing to students and families. Having multiple AP credits may enable students to complete undergraduate work in fewer than four years.

Easy Ways to Raise AP Enrollment

- Host an AP Curriculum Fair to trigger interest and expand access.
- Feature a College Board speaker to explain financial advantages of AP courses.
- Process and highlight AP participation and performance data in visual formats.
- Appoint juniors and seniors as AP outreach ambassadors to middle schools.
- Encourage ninth graders to shadow juniors and seniors in AP classes.
- Involve counselors in identifying underrepresented students with AP potential.
- Invite a college official to explain how AP courses benefit students in the admissions and scholarship processes.
- Find a business patron to sponsor t-shirts that recognize and celebrate AP participation.

Dual Credit Courses

Like AP classes, dual credit courses allow students to earn high school and college credits simultaneously. By performing well in rigorous courses while still in high school, students build confidence to invest the same efforts in college. Also, taking a more demanding schedule in the senior year will help students establish the momentum needed to persist during college.

In many cases, dual credit tuition is reduced compared with normal college costs, which can save students and families thousands of dollars early in the college experience. Students who may have thought college was unaffordable can now see a way to begin.

STORIES FROM EDUCATORS MAKING A DIFFERENCE EACH DAY

The guidance director thought about not picking up the phone at 4:30 p.m. From years of experience, she knew that her counselees would be receiving college notifications today and that wait-listed or rejected students would need consolation. In this phone call, a mother was frantic because her daughter received an admissions rejection from a state college. Should not all state colleges admit capable and hard-working students within that state? The mother had called the college, and the admissions officer explained that test scores were part of the selection criteria. He kindly suggested that her daughter retake the SAT, and she would be reconsidered. Yes, the daughter's SAT score was lower than average, but should one test score impact her admissions status?

SAT and ACT College Admissions Tests

The SAT and ACT are required for the majority of college and university freshman applications, and more students are now taking both exams. College admissions officers use test scores to add to or interpret the high school transcript (The College Board, 2015, p. 26). Grade point averages and difficulty of courses can vary widely from school to school, and standardized test scores offer an objective way for admissions officers to compare college readiness among students.

SAT and ACT school reports give principals and teachers additional student data to use in school improvement efforts and in targeting more direct services to students. School leaders can use the SAT and ACT Discussion Checklist to connect school reporting data with their curriculum, instruction, and assessment work (eResource A). The Checklist will also assist school leaders in providing families with access to basic information about the tests and the many free resources available to their children.

Career and Technical Education

Career and Technical Education (CTE) provides students with the academic and technical programming to give them firsthand knowledge about skills needed for the highly competitive workplace. CTE prepares students for success through real work experiences like shadowing, internships, and mentoring. CTE allows students to earn postsecondary credits through articulated coursework, dual credits, industry-recognized credentials and certifications, and early college programs. CTE has an organizational framework of 16 Career Clusters and 79 related Career Pathways that help students and families better understand career options and the education necessary to find success in these careers (Advance CTE, 2017).

GUIDE TO ACTION

State departments of workforce development have helpful resources about fast growing, high-wage jobs. For example, Hoosier Hot 50 Jobs ranks occupations by salaries and demand for Indiana (2017). Placing these statistics in highly traveled areas will reinforce the message that staying in school is tied to future wages and careers.

Indicators of School Progress toward CTE Readiness

- Increase in students in all CTE classes
- Increase in students completing dual credit courses
- Increase in students earning industry credentials/certificates
- Increase in students participating in shadowing, internships, and mentoring
- Increase in students performing above standard on CTE senior projects
- Increase in students participating in CTE organizations and competitions

School leaders must be prepared to help all students transition beyond K-12 schooling. Understanding the postsecondary credentials and degrees valued in the labor market will assist principals and teachers in designing future-focused classrooms. Knowing more about the academic and technical skills needed by employers will help school leaders direct quality teaching and learning work to adequately prepare students. School leaders who fully understand the many advantages of CTE will be well equipped to guide students toward workplace success.

Eliminate the Distractors

School leaders must remain focused about what matters most, directing students, teachers, and families toward positive outcomes and away from energy-draining special interests. From legislators who use education as a safe platform for re-election to business entrepreneurs who need another market for innovation . . . individuals arrive with quick fixes for school reform. Some come in with the mantra of "we need to make a change" with the same folks not knowing anything about what needs to be changed. Some ideas merit consideration; others not so much. How do school leaders know how to broker the demanding and competing special interests, sorting the good from the bad, for the benefit of students?

RESEARCH TIP

Build Trust with Purposeful and Future-Focused Conversations

Marx (2014) asserts that moving schools forward requires thoughtful discussions about purposes of education. How do we prepare students for becoming good citizens, gaining employability skills, broadening their lives, discovering their abilities and passions, and cultivating their creativity (p. 330)? Marx encourages educators to bring topics forth about what students will need to know and be able to do and place them on a continuing agenda for school and community discussions (p. 330).

School leaders should lead purposeful and future-focused conversations in the school and community. School leaders who are knowledgeable about global trends in context of shaping future citizens will establish trust among stakeholders. Families want to know that schools are prioritizing the critical skills that will enable their children to lead productive and meaningful adult lives. Business and industry leaders want to know that school leaders are

RESEARCH TIP

Seek the Right Drivers for Change and Innovation

Fullan (2014) asserts that school leaders influence student learning best by shaping the environment so that good teaching and learning happens. School leaders need to place primary emphasis on the right drivers of change (capacity building, collaborative effort, pedagogy, and systemness) and weave in the positive aspects of the wrong drivers of change (accountability, individualistic solutions, technology, and fragmented strategies) (pp. 25–26). The wrong drivers can appear as quick solutions, but school leaders should use the right drivers for greater results (p. 26).

assisting students in gaining employability skills. Community members want to know that K-12 students possess the good citizenship skills that will enable them to contribute to a democratic and caring society.

With only so much time and energy, classroom teachers especially depend on school leaders to prevent them from having to participate in fragmented projects lauded as the next silver bullets. Principals and teachers need to maintain their focus on good teaching and learning and not feel guilty for turning down disconnected initiatives. School leaders with strong, future-focused teaching and learning plans can seek a better balance of continuously improving yet minimizing distractions that take away from the school's purpose.

GUIDE TO ACTION

Principals and teachers must stay clear of "Christmas Tree innovations," putting too many glitzy bulbs on the tree or too many unneeded programs in the school. Aggressive vendors are known to set up program demonstrations in the school without checking with the office first. Having frank and frequent conversations with teachers and families about good teaching and learning will result in a well-versed and ready support group for turning away program distractors.

STORIES FROM EDUCATORS MAKING A DIFFERENCE EACH DAY

Experiencing textbook adoption as a school leader is always eye-opening. It may seem exciting at first to receive such enticing emails, but soon the constant barrage of awe-inspiring solutions becomes overwhelming. A software company offers a program demonstration in a tropical climate. A salesperson lists lower prices for participation in a pilot. Another vendor offers free materials if teachers attend pre-demonstration events. One veteran principal, however, quipped, "this is not my first rodeo," and grabbed the leadership reigns to drive textbook adoption himself. This school leader joined teachers in creating and using a rubric, aligned to good teaching and learning, to evaluate textbooks. The school leader responded courteously to vendors that his school was rating products objectively. His adherence to the school's teaching and learning purpose enabled him to turn away all but the highest quality textbook program. With his purposeful guidance, this school leader advocated for greater student outcomes and preserved stakeholder trust.

Principals and teachers must lead with knowledge and urgency to prepare students for success. What young child (if he only knew!) would not find future education and employment challenges intimidating and totally overwhelming? School leaders, teachers, and families must work collaboratively to thoughtfully reject programs that divert time and energy away from quality teaching and learning. Together, principals, teachers, students, and families can focus on what matters most for the benefit of all students.

REFLECTION QUESTIONS

School leaders should ensure that the teaching and learning purpose statement strengthens the school's culture of high expectations. How can we best communicate our teaching and learning purpose to new students, new teachers, and new families? How can we then continue to reinforce the purpose in meaningful ways throughout the school year?

All students need access to core academic content and quality instruction. School leaders should pose simple questions: Do we distribute opportunities to learn fairly? Do we engage in any practices that marginalize any students or student subgroups? How can we provide all students with more access to quality learning and effect positive change?

Since students with growth mindsets have more academic success, school leaders and families need to reflect together about how to send consistent messages about effort. How can we help students see that greater efforts and working hard do matter to future outcomes? How can the school partner with families to encourage practice, multiple attempts, and efforts of learning?

School leaders must help students take advantage of extended day opportunities within their own community. How can the school work in partnership with outside agencies to offer students more chances to engage with intensity in activities of interest to them? How can the school help outside agencies design activities that give students the abilities to make choices and set their own goals?

Principals and teachers should think about how they are preparing students for career pathways most in demand by the labor market. How are we teaching the challenging state academic standards in conjunction with the rigorous career and technical education needed by students? How are we exposing students in all content areas to relevant work-based learning?

School leaders should lead reflection activities about how the school ensures quality as programs are added to the curriculum. How do we determine which programs to keep and which programs to discard? What rubrics should we use to help make the best decisions for our students?

LEADERSHIP TAKE-AWAYS

School leaders should create a focus wall in the main office featuring what matters most for students. Visitors will observe the clear purpose statement that reinforces the school's priority of quality teaching and learning. Newcomers will have first impressions of school leaders who deeply understand the challenges ahead of students.

Principals and teachers should formulate strategies to address digital inequities in homes. Do all families have device and connectivity access to obtain timely school information? Do we send home print copies of important materials for families who cannot access the school website? School leaders should partner with local organizations such as the public library and community centers to expand digital access for families.

Student leaders must reinforce that intelligence is not fixed. When talking with students and families about the state's standardized test scores, school leaders should stress that this is one test that measures skills and abilities at a given point. Sharing the school's other formative assessment measures at the same time will reinforce the belief that students can grow their learning.

Agency and grit are two significant noncognitive factors that lead to student success. Principals and teachers should find new ways to incorporate these factors into teaching and learning plans. Specifically, how can we develop our own schoolwide language and actions to consistently promote grit and agency growth across all classrooms and the school?

School leaders need to empower families with accurate and specific knowledge about college and career targets. For instance, on the SAT, families need to know that students will read informational graphics, such as tables, graphs, and charts, and that vocabulary will be assessed in context of academic and career-related reading. Teachers can then provide families with concrete ways to help their children study and practice at home.

School leaders should create a presentation to share with community groups about the many purposes of education. What do K-12 graduates need to know and be able to do? Principals and teachers can initiate a healthy exchange of ideas about how schools can better prepare students to be productive workers in the global economy and to be good citizens in the local community.

References

Advance CTE: State Leaders Connecting Learning to Work. (2017). Retrieved from https://www.careertech.org/career-clusters

Claro, S., & Paunesku, D. (2014) *Mindset Gap among SES Groups: The Case of Chile with Census Data.* Society for Research on Educational Effectiveness. Retrieved from: https://www.sree.org/conferences/2014f/program/downloads/abstracts/1304.pdf

The College Board. (2015). *Get it together for college: A planner to help you get organized and get in.* New York: Author.

The College Board. (2017). Explore AP. Credit and placement. Retrieved from https://apstudent.collegeboard.org/creditandplacement

Darling-Hammond, L. (2010). *The flat world and education: How America's commitment to equity will determine our future.* New York: Teachers College Press.

Duckworth, A. (2016). *Grit: The power of passion and perseverance.* New York: Scribner.

Duckworth, A.L., Peterson, C., Matthews, M.D., & Kelly, D.R. (2007). Grit: Perseverance and passion for long-term goals. *Journal of Personality and Social Psychology, 92*(6), 1087–1101. doi:10.1037/0022–3514.92.6.1087

Dweck, C. (2006). *Mindset: The new psychology of success.* New York: Ballantine Books.

Every Student Succeeds Act, Public Law 114–95, December 10, 2015; 129 Stat. 1802 (2015).

Farrington, C.A., Roderick, M., Allensworth, E., Nagaoka, J., Keyes, T.S., Johnson, D. W., & Beechum, N.O. (2012). *Teaching adolescents to become learners. The role of noncognitive factors in shaping school performance: A critical literature review.* Chicago: University of Chicago Consortium on Chicago School Research. Retrieved from https://consortium.uchicago.edu/publications/teaching-adolescents-become-learners-role-noncognitive-factors-shaping-school

Felix, A. (2002). *Condi: The Condoleezza Rice story.* New York: Pocket Books.

Fullan, M. (2014). *The principal: Three keys to maximizing impact.* San Francisco: Jossey-Bass.

Hoosier Hot 50 Jobs. (2017). Indiana Department of Workforce Development. Retrieved from https://netsolutions.dwd.in.gov/hh50/

Marzano, R.J., Waters, T., & McNulty, B.A. (2005). *School leadership that works: From research to results.* Alexandria, VA: ASCD.

Marzano, R.J., Warrick, P., & Simms, J.A., with D. Livingston, P. Livingston, F. Pleis, T. Heflebower, J.K. Hoegh, & S. Magaña. (2014). *A handbook for high reliability schools: The next step in school reform.* Bloomington, IN: Marzano Research Laboratory.

Marx, G. (2014). *21 trends for the 21st century: Out of the trenches and into the future.* Bethesda, MD: Education Week Press.

Nagaoka, J., Farrington, C.A., Ehrlich, S.B., Heath, R.D., Johnson, D.W., Dickson, S., Turner, A.C., Mayo, A., & Hayes, K. (2015). *Foundations for young adult success: A developmental framework.* Retrieved from The University of Chicago Consortium on Chicago School Research website: https://consortium.uchicago.edu/sites/default/files/publications/Wallace%20Report.pdf

National Governors Association Center for Best Practices & Council of Chief State School Officers. (2010). Common Core State Standards Development Process. Washington, DC. Retrieved from http://www.corestandards.org/about-the-standards/development-process/

Noguera, P., Darling-Hammond, L., & Friedlaender, D. (2015). *Equal opportunity for deeper learning.* Jobs for the Future. Retrieved from http://www.jff.org/sites/default/files/publications/materials/Equal-Opportunity-for-Deeper-Learning-100115a.pdf

Pink, D. (2009). *Drive: The surprising truth of what motivates us.* New York: Riverhead Books.

Schroeder, A. (2009). *The snowball: Warren Buffett and the business of life.* New York: Bantam Books.

U.S. Department of Education, The Equity and Execellence Commission. (2013). *For each and every child—A strategy for education equity and excellence.*

Washington, D.C. Retrieved from https://www2.ed.gov/about/bdscomm/list/eec/equity-excellence-commission-report.pdf

U.S. Department of Education, National Center for Education Statistics. (2016). *Digest of education statistics.* 2014 (NCES 2016–006). Chapter 3. Retrieved from https://nces.ed.gov/fastfacts/display.asp?id=76

U.S. Department of Education, Office of Educational Technology. (2016). *Future ready learning: Reimagining the role of technology in education.* Retrieved from http://tech.ed.gov

Whitaker, T. (2010). *The ball.* Bloomington, IN: Triple Nickel Press.

Zinth, J. (2016). Education Commission of the States. Response to Information Request. Retrieved from www.ecs.org

Lead Learning
with Easy Data Use

Simple Strategies

- ■ Shape a Culture of Inquiry
- ■ Lead with a Collaborative Data Protocol
- ■ Connect Teacher Learning to Student Learning
- ■ Celebrate Student Performance and Growth
- ■ Engage Families in Interactive Data Activities

In a school with a streamlined teaching and learning plan, working with data is just how they do business. First graders are plotting school days present with accompanying illustrations of reasons for days missed. Fourth graders are practicing chart-reading skills of bus arrival and departure schedules as a principal/teacher action research team documents student engagement. Fifth graders are color-coding bar graphs of three-year trend performances for upcoming student-led family conferences. Eighth graders are exploring careers and rank ordering salary and education requirements to take home and engage families in further discussions. Tenth graders are digging into college admissions data and comparing profiles of accepted students. Here, the principal, teachers, students, and families are using data seamlessly within their teaching and learning plan.

ESSENTIAL QUESTION

HOW DO SCHOOL LEADERS USE DATA STRATEGICALLY AND EASILY TO ENHANCE THE QUALITY OF TEACHING AND ACHIEVE GREATER STUDENT OUTCOMES?

In the above vignette, data are hardly overwhelming and intimidating for school leaders; in fact, a closer inspection reveals quite the opposite. School leaders have grabbed the reins and are using data in powerful ways for greater student and school improvement. Where data use is embedded throughout good teaching and learning, school leaders are not fretting excessively about testing mandates and accountability reports. Instead of viewing data as isolated add-ons to daily work, principals and teachers believe data are all-important components within the instructional day. In strategic planning all year long, principals and teachers are making the right choices to collect only that data most relevant to students' needs, most useful to classroom instruction, and most informative for keeping the school on track toward continuous improvement.

Data enable principals and teachers to gain fresh insight about students and the school. Data are who we are and who we want to become. Meaningful data plus powerful practitioner knowledge and practices are the right combinations for bringing about positive change. To ensure that all students have opportunities to reach higher college, career, and life goals, principals and teachers must track student progress incrementally using rich data sources. Data are effective and energizing forces for building momentum toward a learning culture.

GUIDE TO ACTION

Sometimes, when spoken at educational conferences, *data* is that "D" word that brings out moans and groans while others leave the room to get coffee. Instead of passively regarding data as something "being done" to them for random accountability reasons, principals and teachers need to use data to their advantage. Scheduling regular data discussions will lead to discoveries of new ways that data use can benefit student and school growth.

Principals and teachers must be self-assured and data-ready. School leaders who model the importance of data will influence others to embrace data use. Yes, students and families are critical data partners, but principals and teachers must ambitiously set the tone of high expectations for data use. When data use is woven throughout a healthy learning culture, staff members' attitudes about the benefits of using data trumps ability to crunch numbers every time. School leaders do not need to be doctoral level statisticians, yet they must be able to rally others around using data as part of the school's common language of good teaching and learning.

RESEARCH TIP

School Leaders Should Understand Assessment Purposes

Popham (2016) categorizes assessments into primary purposes: (1) Comparing test takers (includes state tests that sort students by performances); (2) Improving instruction (includes formative tests that assist teachers in adjusting instruction; and (3) Evaluating instruction (includes summative assessments that document quality of instruction) (pp. 47–48).

School leaders who couple a positive attitude about data use with the *why* and the *how* of assessments are ready to lead. School leaders need to understand the purposes for creating and using assessments as well as how to best connect data to improvement results. Random acts of data use will not help anyone. Excessive data are descending upon schools, and pared down, deliberate data use is smart data use. School leaders can then act on the right data and ignore the rest.

Shape a Culture of Inquiry

Conceptualizing data use will be a wise investment of time and energy. Principals and teachers should think strategically about what data are

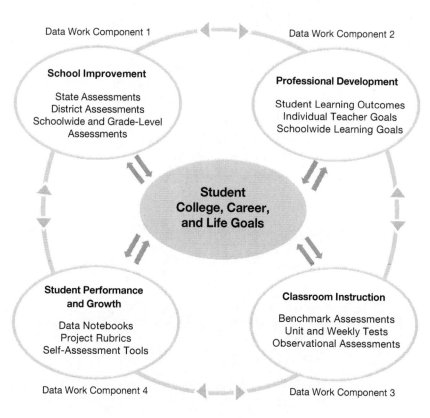

Figure 2.1 Data Work Conceptualization Model

needed and why, and they will build background knowledge together. Having that common understanding and language will not only help with the practical aspect of streamlining data work, but it will also bolster teamwork within the school culture. Data work in schools can easily be grouped into four major components: school improvement, professional development, classroom instruction, and student performance and growth.

School Improvement (Data Work Component 1)

At the school level, data work centers on organizational effectiveness. Principals and teachers use multiple measures to set ambitious goals and objectives for student and school success. Data reveal answers to questions about how students are progressing toward goals and keep teachers informed as to how to modify instruction to best meet the goals.

Guiding questions might include: Are all students making progress toward college and career targets? Are students improving in performance and growth toward state standards and local curriculum? Here, principals and teachers are looking at overall student outcomes across the school and across grade levels, making comparisons with prior years and examining patterns. Data reveal progress toward goals by overall students and subgroup performances. What are the strengths, opportunities, and gaps in achievement that need to be addressed within school improvement work? Achievement gaps are further examined by student assistance teams to identify and address root causes of student learning problems.

Data Types that Inform School Improvement

State assessments are standardized measures, developed by testing companies, that document student progress consistently across districts and schools. Schools benchmark annual progress and make comparisons with schools of similar demographics. State assessments are used to determine student performance and growth for accountability purposes. Schools and families use year end performance and growth trend data to monitor student progress on grade level standards toward graduation.

ESSA's Guidance about State Assessments

- Assessments measure student progress against challenging state academic standards.
- Assessments include at least three levels of achievement.
- Reading or language arts, math, and science are measured.
- Assessments are aligned to higher education and career and technical standards.
- Assessments include multiple measures to assess higher-order thinking skills and understanding.
- Assessments report progress of all students and subgroups on academic indicators.

(ESSA, 2015)

RESEARCH TIP

Challenging State Assessments Ready Students for Global Workforce

Darling-Hammond (2014) finds that rigorous assessments have improved measures of deeper learning skills and real-world applications needed for the global workforce. The development of assessments aligned to Common Core State Standards is a positive step toward higher-level learning, but leaders must also use these assessments effectively (2014, p. 36).

District assessments are locally developed or purchased assessments administered across schools. The assessments provide a picture of school and grade level performance against local curriculum, including state standards. District assessments are given in accordance to pacing guides and are likely administered at quarter, semester, or year-end intervals. More disaggregated data about student performance and growth toward mastery of local curriculum and state standards enable timely adjustments to be made in pacing guides and curricular materials. School leaders can more closely monitor achievement gaps that persist among grades or subgroups.

Schoolwide and grade level assessments provide a comprehensive picture of teaching and learning in action. Teacher teams at various grade levels administer pre-determined assessments, such as unit and weekly tests, to benchmark incremental learning. These assessments show whether students are keeping pace with other students in mastering local curriculum. The resulting data are especially valuable for designing schoolwide and grade level remediation and enrichment programs.

Professional Development (Data Work Component 2)

Figure 2.1 shows the important connection of adult learning to school improvement, classroom instruction, and student performance and growth. Teachers desire training in data use that will lead to greater student learning outcomes. Setting individual teacher goals will more closely tie data collection to designing strategies to improve classroom instruction.

Working toward progress on schoolwide learning goals will promote collegial learning and improve the capacity of the school as a whole to better meet student needs.

Data Types that Inform Professional Development

Student learning outcomes are opportunities for teacher training. Before teachers can think about schoolwide or their own professional needs, they must know more about the *why* of daily student learning. What cognitive skills and noncognitive factors will best prepare students for college and the workplace? What outcomes are important to students, and how will the school measure progress toward those outcomes? To illustrate, with ESSA's (2015) requirement of challenging state academic standards, teachers are eager to understand the state assessment blueprint around the standards. What are the expectations for students in reading complex text? How are our students performing on the higher levels of reading standards? How can we help students build the reading stamina that they will need? What writing rubric is used for grading on the state assessment? Are the writing process components or the writing conventions criteria given more emphasis? How do we help students persist in producing the quantity of writing that is expected?

GUIDE TO ACTION

Teachers want to learn more about how they can help all students be successful. Data analysis of student learning must include a focus on equity. Principals and teachers must lead meetings with pointed questions: What do the data tell us about performance and growth of our student subgroups? What are we doing to address achievement gaps among these subgroups? What differentiated supports are we providing to ensure all students are achieving to their full potential?

Individual teacher goals enable teachers to increase their own professional growth. At the beginning of the year, teachers set evaluation and/or other professional improvement goals and determine ways that they will measure the goals. In looking at student needs, what aspects of my professional work need to be strengthened to better help students? Engaging in research, individual learning modules, and applications of varying strategies around the goal topics will enhance learning. For many teachers, watching peers in action is most effective. For example, one teacher may hear about how another teacher is using a certain evidence-based strategy effectively with low performing students. When a colleague observes another teacher with pre-determined questions, both teachers can then reflect on the objective responses and learn together. Professional learning logs or reflection journals are helpful in collecting peer observation data and documenting individual teacher growth.

RESEARCH TIP

Student Data Drive Teacher Professional Development

Perlman and Redding (2011) convey guidance to states, districts, and schools about evidence-based practices that bring about quick improvements in low performing schools. One action principle involves using student data to improve instruction, which includes training principals and teachers in analyzing and using formative data (Perlman & Redding, 2011, p. 113). Other action principles promote using data to change classroom practices through teacher research/study teams and coaching cohorts (Perlman & Redding, 2011, p. 117).

Schoolwide learning goals allow principals and teachers to engage in ongoing learning and assess progress toward goals. What schoolwide goals do we need to set based upon our student data, and what professional development opportunities will help us improve toward these goals? Principal and teacher focus groups are instrumental in driving the learning. For instance, during faculty meetings, teachers can respond to open-ended questions about the effectiveness of classroom strategies. As you observe students, what instructional strategies are having the most effect? How could we structure professional development to strengthen these strategies and make them more widespread? And, within various content areas and at different grade levels, what professional development opportunities would most impact student learning? To illustrate, teachers may suggest vertical team meetings to share data and better scaffold learning between grades. School leaders should seek feedback about what types of professional development forums, such as content or pedagogy workshops, modeling and coaching, professional learning communities, or individual e-learning would best bolster schoolwide learning.

Classroom Instruction (Data Work Component 3)

Classroom data use is about meeting instructional needs of students. Teachers utilize multiple measures to monitor each student's progress toward local curriculum and school improvement goals. Using data, teachers make frequent decisions to alter classroom instruction, changing daily practices in order to engage all students and address individual needs. By monitoring classroom data closely and regularly, teachers ensure that all students have opportunities to learn, that principles of equity are observed for all students, and that differentiation and enrichment activities are yielding improvements.

RESEARCH TIP

Formative Assessment Raises Achievement

Black and Wiliam (1998) conducted an extensive literature review of 250 articles and chapters and found that formative assessment raises achievement standards (p. 140). Researchers concluded that significant formative assessment work in classrooms is the best way they know to raise standards (p. 148). Bangert-Drowns, Kulik, and Kulik (1991) analyzed 29 studies and also found that higher achievement is correlated with frequency of assessments and that giving regular assessments leads to a more positive classroom environment (pp. 97–98).

Data Types that Inform Classroom Instruction

Benchmark assessments document student progress toward goals and objectives in mastering local curriculum. For instance, early literacy measures track individual and group performances toward improved reading skills in phonemic awareness, phonics, fluency, vocabulary, and comprehension. Data on benchmark assessments are particularly useful in assisting teachers in grouping students to practice identified skills.

GUIDE TO ACTION

Dynamic Indicators of Basic Early Literacy Skills (DIBELS) are examples of benchmark assessments that principals and teachers use to track early reading progress (University of Oregon, 2017). How frustrating it can be for families to hear that their children are struggling with reading but little helpful feedback is provided. Instead, during family conferences, teachers can share progress on specific benchmarks like DIBELS oral reading fluency, along with suggested practice activities, so that families can help students strengthen specific reading skills at home.

Unit and weekly tests help teachers determine what students have and have not learned before deciding to proceed in instruction. Unit and weekly tests add more knowledge about whether students are making necessary progress on local curriculum as listed on district pacing guides. Item-analysis reports assist teachers in identifying key errors and determining which areas to reteach in different ways.

Observational assessments are quick and effective tools that translate classroom data into better teaching and learning. As teachers use daily routines, they watch students and note skills mastered. To illustrate, in primary grades, teachers can observe and easily assess oral counting skills, obtaining immediate results and saving time from grading paperwork. Even in large groups, teachers can quickly observe students who struggle and intervene with necessary supports.

RESEARCH TIP

Quick Data Give Better Feedback for Teaching and Learning

In their research on high reliability schools, Marzano et al. (2014) document the significance of using data in day-to-day teaching and learning. They liken the logistics of a school to the workings of an aircraft carrier where data collection and observation are critical in preventing errors (p. 7). The researchers support gathering easily accessible data in conversations and observations for ensuring top performance. Quick data enable school leaders to celebrate positive feedback in a timely manner (Marzano et al., 2014, p.11).

STORIES FROM EDUCATORS MAKING A DIFFERENCE EACH DAY

Joining a kindergarten math lesson is always an adventure. While sitting on a colorful learning mat with the class, I watched a kindergarten teacher and her students examine algebraic relationships. The teacher led students in patterning chants while students manipulated objects to demonstrate their understanding. The teacher quickly recorded formative data about her students' mathematical thinking on her class chart. For instance, the teacher noted that Ava recognized repeating patterns involving colors, but she did not recognize repeating patterns using shapes. The teacher quickly put checks in columns on the chart to document which students needed more targeted practice with which pattern attributes, such as colors, shapes, or sizes. To celebrate their diligent work, the teacher cheerfully urged kindergartners to give themselves brain kisses! Formative assessment data were well-aligned and useful pieces that led to greater outcomes in this kindergarten classroom.

Student Performance and Growth (Data Work Component 4)

At appropriate developmental levels, students should understand the expected local curriculum including the state standards. Students should be able to state their own goals and show their progress toward those goals. Principals and teachers need to give students structured ways to track performance and growth in order to better visualize their own process of learning.

Data Types that Inform Student Performance and Growth

Data notebooks encourage students to track their own progress toward goals. As students compile their own data, they better comprehend their relevance. For example, students may chart three year trend data of English, math, and science progress on state assessments, noting performance and growth in varying content areas on specific standards. By drawing the charts themselves in their notebooks, students see that they are responsible for their own data. And, asking students to write data narratives to accompany their charts further motivates them to take ownership of their progress.

Data notebooks are especially beneficial in helping students make the right choices in their learning. School leaders can direct students to track other data that impact teaching and learning, such as attendance, tardies, and discipline referrals so that students can identify root causes of problem areas and make better decisions.

Project rubrics clarify student learning guidelines. When teachers use rubrics in advance to convey requirements on classroom assignments, students can better calibrate how to organize the work. Students can then more accurately adjust time and seek out assistance where needed. Understanding the criteria that distinguish an "outstanding" from a "very good" project is a positive motivator for students as they discover how to expend more energy and effort to perform at higher levels.

Self-assessment tools enable students to better evaluate their own choices in the learning process. As students complete units and lessons, self-assessment tools force students to look more closely at all aspects of completed tasks and take responsibility for outcomes at the various work stages. Students reflect on strengths as well as opportunities missed in creating quality work products. For example, when students use self-assessment tools as they are working on performance tasks, they pay attention to details in enough time to catch up, make necessary changes, and then find success before finishing the tasks. In this way, self-assessment tools are effective in promoting equitable learning opportunities.

Teachers can design basic questions that encourage students' self-reflection about their work.

Easy Self-Assessment Questions (While Completing a Task)

- What is the purpose of the work? Am I achieving that purpose?
- Am I following directions carefully?
- Does each step of my work flow smoothly into the next?
- Am I checking my work for mistakes?
- Can I improve on any aspect of my work?

Data Literacy and Inquiry

The Data Work Conceptualization Model (Figure 2.1) illustrates the dynamic interplay of school improvement, professional development, classroom instruction, and student performance and growth work in deepening a culture of inquiry. Principals and teachers are heard in hallways chatting about data: I am anxious to see if my small group work makes any difference on the unit test. Or, I am hoping to see gains in reading scores after our intensive vocabulary study. Or, did you see Tamika's data notebook where she graphed non-fiction books read this grading period?

Data literacy training should focus on school, classroom, and student levels, depending on identified priorities. Years of classroom experience should not indicate need for data literacy training. As awareness for data training has become evident, many colleges and universities have more recently added the component into preservice training. Thus, younger teachers may have had more advanced training in data use, and many veteran teachers may now welcome additional training. Informally surveying teachers as to data literacy needs will enable school leaders to structure the most beneficial professional development forums. And, the initial training will hopefully lead to further areas of data interest and inquiry. School leaders can use Data Literacy Discussion Questions to engage teachers in more focused dialogue about data use (eResource B).

Lead with a Collaborative Data Protocol

With a Data Work Conceptualization Model and common language about data in place, school leaders are ready to mobilize others and create the school's own data protocol. Guiding teachers through the development of a Collaborative Data Protocol is a significant and high-yield professional development activity. Although it may sound time intensive, the process actually streamlines and simplifies data use, focusing energy and actions in a systematic way throughout the year. The collaborative

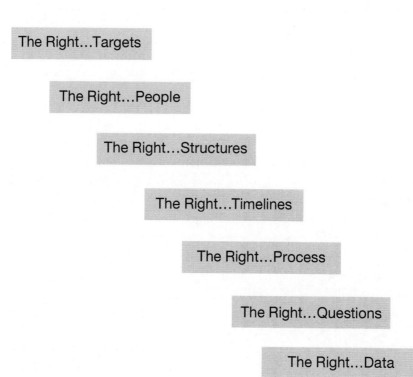

Figure 2.2 Promising Recipe for a Collaborative Data Protocol

component is crucial as the schoolwide process must belong to the principal, teachers, students, and families if it is to become part of daily teaching and learning. Growing the school's own data protocol will build awareness, trust, and motivation to use the protocol to make lasting improvements. By devising the protocol together and strengthening interrelated data components, there is a much greater likelihood that meaningful data use will move beyond compliance and become embedded in the culture of the school.

A Collaborative Data Protocol needs the right ingredients.

The Right . . . Targets

When school leaders focus on the right college and career targets, they reduce anxiety and ensure clarity about important components that contribute to the definition of student success. From kindergarten to Grade 12, principals and teachers make choices as to what learning opportunities will be presented to students. Time and resources are precious commodities that educators allocate, and they must make informed and calculated decisions to serve all students fairly and most effectively. Having a shared understanding about the right targets will expand ownership for learning and increase motivation to focus on what matters.

School leaders need to review local curriculum in all content areas. This is not a cursory yearly review but instead a coordinated, ongoing look at what skills and abilities students will need at all grade levels to progress toward college and career targets. How do we best help students develop the cognitive and noncognitive abilities they will need to meet the challenges ahead? School leaders need to continuously research the makeup of the targets and the pathways of learning necessary for students to reach the targets. What an exciting journey for principals and teachers as they learn together as a school team so that students can be best prepared!

The Right . . . People

Principals, teachers, students, and families are the main ingredients within the Collaborative Data Protocol. Data illuminate the forward flow of the school; they tell us to what degree students are making progress, but people with knowledge and passion give life to the numbers, spreadsheets, charts, and graphs. When school leaders ask questions about data, others will see transparency in learning and its advantages in helping all students improve performance and growth.

The Right People . . . most certainly include students and families. Collectively thinking about data together is a powerful practice, and school leaders must seek out novel ways to work alongside families to make connections between data and learning. When principals and teachers are passionate and purposeful about data, families will want to join the team.

STORIES FROM EDUCATORS MAKING A DIFFERENCE EACH DAY

Joining a four-week curriculum auditing course was beneficial to me as a new director of curriculum and instruction. Measuring teaching and learning against high quality operational standards and using data to accelerate educational productivity were topics that intrigued me. Process efficiency was a term used repeatedly by the auditing specialists that helped me rethink tighter connections among curriculum, instruction, and assessment. I left the seminar with a curriculum auditing certification and a much better understanding of organizational effectiveness. However, as I brought this information back to my district, I quickly realized that the data alignment processes had to be relevant to our schools and classrooms. Working with numbers in an isolated seminar room was not the same as working with numbers in context with real students with varying needs. School leaders need to recognize the importance of merging processes and people to truly bring about student and school improvement.

The Right . . . Structures

The school infrastructure is key to using data most effectively and efficiently to impact teaching and learning. Where and during what forums do teachers, students, and families meet to discuss data-related issues? When school leaders regularly schedule meetings for data collection and analysis, they can ensure that the right people will be brought together in productive ways to measure student progress.

GUIDE TO ACTION

An exciting aspect of the collaborative data protocol is that principals and teachers can design their own structured settings to capture data. Perhaps the first 15 minutes of each faculty meeting is designated to look at student work. Each grade level or department can alternate in leading discussions about their criteria for success.

Having data discussions during multiple and diverse forums ensures that the school prioritizes data decision making throughout the year. No longer will the end of the year meeting center on data review; instead, data seamlessly and continuously inform instructional activities.

Examples of Data Discussion Forums

Faculty meetings

Grade level groups

Teacher team meetings

School improvement workshops

Instructional coach sessions

Counselor meetings

Special education conferences

Principal advisory groups

Professional development sessions

Student/teacher/family conferences

The Right . . . Timelines

None of the other Collaborative Data Protocol ingredients are likely to make an impact if the school's data work does not include well-communicated timelines. Early in the year, school leaders should publish calendars for teachers and families that list ongoing state, district, and school assessments. Having pacing guides with designated timelines for data collection helps principals and teachers ensure that meaningful data work is spread throughout the year.

School leaders must leverage opportunities at regular meetings as well as carve out periods during the school day for data work and collaborative conversations. "We don't have time" is not a valid excuse when data work is embedded into the daily work, language, and culture of the school.

STORIES FROM EDUCATORS MAKING A DIFFERENCE EACH DAY

State officials regularly visit low-performing schools. The well-meaning state officials sometimes bring data protocol brochures, yet the guidelines about using the protocols are often disjointed and overwhelming. However, when a school embraces data use as part of good teaching and learning, as opposed to top-down compliance, exciting changes begin to take place. In one instance, I watched a principal and teachers craft a data protocol, from the ground up, and it became their own. They had much data already, but institutionalizing a process for data collection, analysis, and reflection was game-changing. Taking a proactive approach that would be most valuable to students, they developed their own procedures and timelines for use of data boards, data notebooks, teacher team rounds, and family forums. Data use became uplifting and a source of pride.

The Right . . . Process

Having consistent and well-known data use procedures in place encourages collaboration and productivity. Robust data use becomes a habit for principals, teachers, students, and families.

Data use is integral to continuous school improvement, and school leaders need to ensure that the process follows basic agreed-upon assumptions. Principals and teachers should collectively devise their own assumptions about teaching and learning and the importance of data to the process. Principals and teachers should brainstorm together and spell out their own beliefs about schoolwide data use.

Sample Assumptions about Data Use

- Data set direction for overall continuous school improvement.
- Data inform teaching and learning practices at the school and classroom levels.
- Data motivate students to be self-directed learners.

- Data should direct professional learning of the principal and teachers.
- Data should be shared with families to keep them informed of student learning progress.

The Right . . . Questions

Having a Collaborative Data Protocol will embed continuous inquiry into the school's culture. Principals, teachers, students, and families need to have open forums for asking questions and for making everyone knowledgeable and comfortable about data inquiry. In developing the protocol, principals and teachers should generate basic teaching and learning questions that can be repeated over time and within various structures. And, excitement and enthusiasm for data use will build when questions generate other clarifying questions that require more exploration and subsequent data collection and investigation.

Basic Teaching and Learning Questions

- What do our students need to learn?
- How will that learning be assessed and measured?
- What interventions will be put in place to address gaps in student learning?
- How will learning be supported and extended through next steps?

The Right . . . Data

Data-agile principals, teachers, students, and families look at student outcomes persistently throughout the school year, drilling down to specific needs and making better decisions about learning priorities. Having a Collaborative Data Protocol focused on the right data reduces distraction and keeps the momentum going toward improvement that matters.

Reviewing a variety of quantitative and qualitative data will provide a clearer picture of teaching and learning. Although most school improvement processes tend to focus on quantitative data, such as test scores and multiple choice surveys, school leaders also need to include rich qualitative data, such as, open-ended questions and interviews. Focus groups are easy and reliable ways to capture meaningful feedback to make incremental program changes. The right data are those powerful pieces that uncover areas of need and add fresh perspectives and insight for student and school improvement.

Connect Teacher Learning to Student Learning

Connecting teacher learning to student learning around rich data use advances a strong culture of inquiry. Student learning expectations have been greatly accelerated, and principals and teachers have opportunities like never before to engage in professional learning around the higher levels of assessments and twenty-first-century workplace skills. The Collaborative Data Protocol is a ready source of clear processes and plentiful data to drive teacher learning in new ways. Principals and teachers should seize the most useful data and devise the most beneficial learning opportunities. Being co-learners in making meaning around data use will be revitalizing and morale-boosting for principals and teachers.

STORIES FROM EDUCATORS MAKING A DIFFERENCE EACH DAY

Serving on a community hospital board has re-energized me to look more closely for improvement opportunities in data gathering, analysis, and reflection. Hospital quality experts spend significant time and energy in reviewing and learning from data, and I have been impressed and inspired with their positive and open attitudes about data use. Integral to the medical culture, regular data review is an expected, ongoing practice, and data points are viewed as future opportunities. By reviewing quality metrics to enhance patient care collaboratively during multiple forums, hospital personnel take ownership in the results and pride in the positive outcomes that result over time. Reviewing data regularly and having frequent and candid internal dialogue builds momentum for future gains.

School leaders should distribute responsibilities of building the school's knowledge base and of monitoring data about the postsecondary and workplace challenges ahead. Teacher experts can provide key leadership in keeping other teachers informed and students on track toward success. When teachers spend time researching and working with data, they stretch their own abilities and contribute to the school's collective learning culture.

School leaders can effectively link teacher learning to student learning with college and career target study teams and classroom data action teams.

College and Career Target Study Teams

College and career target study teams are examples of structures within the Collaborative Data Protocol that inspire adult learning while also bringing about greater student outcomes. Reviewing data in context of the real challenges ahead for students attaches meaning and relevance to the learning.

Principals and teachers can select different college and career targets and begin! (See College and Career Targets, Figure 1.1.) In study teams, principals and teachers become in-house experts about target expectations, and, on an ongoing basis, update colleagues about critical information and about student progress on the targets. How exciting for all teachers to learn more from the study team about Advanced Placement courses and about the progression of knowledge students will need to be successful in those courses!

After schoolwide sharing, team members may reach out to others during small group or paired discussions to further analyze data, ask more questions, or seek input for curriculum changes. College and career target study teams will continue to be responsible for monitoring data about postsecondary and work challenges and integrating new knowledge into the continuous improvement process.

Classroom Data Action Teams

Real opportunities exist for teacher learning and instructional improvements through classroom data action teams. Teachers are enthusiastic about data they can use right away. Classrooms immediately become evidence-rich laboratories for studying real-time student performance and growth.

Having classroom data action teams as part of the Collaborative Data Protocol ensures that data closest to student levels will inform ongoing school improvement.

Classroom data action teams give principals and teachers options in data collection. Having choice will increase the likelihood that principals and teachers will be motivated to use data in thoughtful, new ways. And, receiving evidence-based feedback from colleagues enables teachers to refine and adjust teaching practices with confidence.

Classroom data action teams offer benefits of originality and flexibility. Teams can find new ways to collect data that currently exist in classrooms as opposed to creating unnecessary assessments. What would we like to learn about our current instructional practices? How are these practices impacting student outcomes? Several topics will likely emerge as possibilities for data analysis, and then principals and teachers can decide which topics are most valuable to impact student learning.

GUIDE TO ACTION

Adult learning about data use should be all about keeping it cutting-edge, fresh, and meaningful. Studying data and professional materials together builds fellowship and increases job satisfaction. A possible study resource is *The Principal as Assessment Leader* (Guskey, [Ed.], 2009), which includes a compilation of assessment insights for principal and teacher learning.

Classroom data action teams can devise their own data-friendly, internal review tools. For instance, classroom audits of instructional strategies provide teachers with better knowledge about the implementation of strategies across the school. Audits show frequencies of strategies and applications in different content areas. Effectiveness of strategy use with varying student groups is also obtained. Teams can record observations across grade levels and content areas. Reporting formats emerge that are most useful for colleagues to inform school improvement work.

Classroom data action teams should triangulate data to ensure validity and reliability of results. Besides the classroom audit of instructional strategies, the combination of peer observation and teacher focus groups can provide three powerful data points about the effectiveness of instructional strategies. Looking for patterns that emerge in the predicted and/or unexpected data stimulates good conversation that is integral to the data analysis process. Are we providing all students with the very best opportunities to learn?

Time spent discussing classroom data and needed next steps leads principals and teachers to new ways of thinking and a deeper understanding of good teaching. Classroom data analysis work not only assists teachers in making data-supported modifications to classroom practices, but the process also validates their abilities as a faculty team to improve teaching and learning. Their unified voices add a level of rigor to data work. Principals and teachers are contributing to a vital and reflective culture of awesome teaching and learning.

Celebrate Student Performance and Growth

What if . . . instead of waiting for accountability mandates to descend upon them, school leaders showcased their own expertise in how students in their classrooms and schools were making higher levels of performance and growth? To do this, school leaders need a solid understanding of the high-stakes definitions. For school improvement and state accountability purposes, what is meant by student performance and growth?

Student performance is measured against content standards on state assessments, primarily in English/language arts, mathematics, and science. ESSA (2015) requires each state to report three levels of student performance, likely whether students are at, above, or below mastery levels. Disaggregation reports compare passing rates for overall students and subgroups for the state, districts, schools, and grade levels.

Growth in accountability systems continues to generate interest. Statistical growth models determine how much change in test scores is equal to one year of student learning. Growth models focus attention on individual and student group progress over time and reveal where, and among which students, and with which teachers, the strongest growth is happening. Students may be classified into low, medium, and high categories, and growth is tracked from one year to the next in comparison with similar students.

Student performance and growth definitions are largely about progress in academic content areas. Principals and teachers need to be aware that definitions of performance and growth are limited and just part of student development. However, as leaders of schools and classrooms, they also know that many college and career targets are centered on the English/language arts, mathematics, and science content areas. Students deserve school leaders who prioritize equity and opportunities to learn, enabling them to develop the needed academic and critical learning skills and abilities to be successful in higher education, work, and life.

Student Data Document Performance and Growth

Multiple formative assessments give teachers the needed data to bring about greater student performance and growth. Each day, teachers gather information in structured and informal ways to diagnose where students are performing in relation to specific skills and abilities. School leaders should fully utilize the many different types of formative assessments.

Local Curriculum Assessments

Textbooks and supplementary materials have a wealth of quality, ready-made formative assessments that are closely aligned with the core content. Teachers use assessment handbooks and digital products to pace classroom learning, determining how students are progressing in regard to specific skills and abilities. Teachers can easily modify formative assessments to look more closely at gaps in student understanding. Check tests are often used throughout lessons so that teachers can pinpoint incremental progress, give specific feedback, and then reteach areas of misunderstanding.

Performance Assessments

Performance assessments make expectations crystal-clear for students. Students understand assignment expectations and can set goals and monitor progress toward those goals. When students are unsure about what steps to take next, they can refer back to the clear criteria, self-reflect, and adjust their work efficiently. For instance, assignment criteria might show students that to earn a rating of "excellent," their work must include at least three pieces of evidence to support their arguments.

When teachers use performance-based assessment tools, they reinforce growth-oriented thinking. All students are capable of quality work if they are willing to put forth the time, energy, and quality needed. As students become more adept at monitoring their progress against known criteria, they better perceive the correlation between effort and high quality performance.

Formative Classroom Conversations

Teacher guiding and coaching can greatly impact student performance and growth. Pre-and post-assessments are frequently used, but, formative classroom conversations, which take place during learning, can be the ones that most influence active learning. Listening and observing students closely as they engage during lessons enables teachers to share in their learning. Conversations with students give teachers greater insight about how students are thinking as they perform tasks. Discussing the rationale for particular actions enables students to process thinking. Teachers can then make more precise inferences and share more useful feedback. Classroom conversations not only enable teachers to better advise students about possible next steps, but they also motivate students to act on the lessons they learned themselves.

Guiding Questions for Formative Classroom Conversations

- What intentional strategies did you use in your work?
- Why did you choose these strategies?
- Did the strategies work for you?
- How do you know that you improved with your strategy choices?
- How can you bring about more growth with different strategies in the future?

Student Focus Groups

Student focus groups at the classroom and school levels provide essential perspectives about performance and growth. As an example, school leaders can structure open-ended dialogue with students about progress toward school improvement goals. Hearing student voices adds the important dimension of reality to school improvement taking place within classrooms across the school. Students' unabridged conversations add a true picture of learning. School leaders can then reflect: What new or surprising perspectives about learning did the students share? How can principals and teachers take action on the formative feedback? What insights need further clarification and study?

Student Data Displays

Data displays are informal ways to build shared ownership around student performance and growth. User-friendly data boards in highly visible areas will raise data awareness and communicate the school's dedication to measuring student progress. Visuals engage a variety of audiences in data analysis and encourage conversations about school improvement.

Surrounding stakeholders with the right data in the most helpful formats such as charts, tables, and graphs will make data easier to comprehend. For instance, bar graphs would be effective in showing percentages of students achieving mastery of state standards at the varying grade levels and within different content areas. A scatter chart (colored bubbles) might better illustrate the relationship between two different measures such as student performance and growth. And a pie chart illustrates part-to-whole distributions such as a breakdown of all students in the school who scored at the advanced level of mastery, adequate level of mastery, or low level of mastery on the state assessment. A focusing question at the top of the display reinforces the purpose for collecting the data and piques curiosity for viewers to discuss causality.

Student data displays are tremendous learning opportunities. By creating the visuals themselves, students of all ages will become better consumers of data and more involved in their own improvement.

Easy Ways to Display Student Performance and Growth

- Students write about and post ways that they have accomplished daily objectives.

- Students track evidence of homework completed by the class.
- Students draw concept maps that highlight main areas of their learning.
- Students post reports of response systems (such as clickers) that show learning.
- Students illustrate three words that represent main ideas of their learning.
- Students post answers to questions using sticky notes.

Engage Families in Interactive Data Activities

Data use draws families into schools! When school leaders open family meetings with a data focus, they build collective responsibility for improved student outcomes. Families care about their children and value healthy relationships with principals and teachers that emphasize a commitment to ongoing student progress. When school leaders begin with data, they have an excellent rallying point for initiating productive conversations.

School leaders must empower families with knowledge about assessment data. Families must better understand formative and summative assessments and their roles in helping their children make significant changes in performance and growth. School leaders must be specific about the purposes of state and classroom assessments and show examples. When families better understand the differences behind the many assessments, they can be more active partners in helping to track progress of their children's learning.

Communication about student learning must be reciprocal. Families are excellent resources for principals and teachers to solicit feedback about student learning styles and work habits at home. Principals and teachers can glean more about how students are viewed by families in terms of strengths and opportunities for learning. Do students have positive attitudes about homework? Why or why not? How can the school help students acquire good study habits that extend into their homes?

College and Career Target Awareness Seminars

Families will attend school meetings about their children's futures! Families depend on school leaders to apprise them about expectations ahead and about ways to support their children. The targets have changed since parents and grandparents were in school so updates about target timelines, make-up, and relevance are crucial. Having a teacher team present research and updated information about the various targets will keep families informed and energized about helping their children move forward.

School leaders need to keep school and family forums interactive. Having the data already processed and in visual formats will help organize meetings so that two-way discussions can take place. Shared understanding provides a foundation for an ongoing exchange of conversation and ideas among principals, teachers, and families. As educators and families learn more about the college and career targets together, they can more accurately set and monitor goals for students.

Student-Led Family Data Conferences

Families want to see and hear their children talk about data. Data use is most impactful to families when students are the data producers and consumers. Student-led conferences are excellent forums within the collaborative data protocol that empower students to take responsibility for their learning.

Allowing students to take the lead in sharing data with families will help improve their oral communication skills as well as build their self-confidence. Asking students to begin with their learning goals enables families and teachers to be on the same page with expectations. Students can use data notebooks to highlight progress on state assessments and school and classroom formative assessments. And, encouraging students to talk about the mistakes they have made can stimulate healthy dialogue and strengthen that important growth mindset. Together, principals, teachers, and families can celebrate evidence of improvement and guide students to understand that sustained efforts lead to success.

Student and Family Transition Meetings

What if students and families were invited to data conferences at the beginning of the school year to co-design an action plan for the upcoming year? Instead of starting over each year, principals, teachers, students, and families should meet early in the year to review student work and create goals for the upcoming year. Student-focused school and family teams can use data to identify student strengths and learning needs and talk about roles in assisting students as the year unfolds. Having a partnership of supporters from the onset will be motivating for students. School leaders should pose guiding questions: What skills and abilities did students develop last year that most helped them in the learning? What new goals should students set for the upcoming year? And, what supports will be most useful in the upcoming year to bolster more learning?

Family Data Celebrations

Families want to join student accomplishment and data celebrations! Leveraging lively and fun events such as celebratory breakfasts, luncheons, or dinners to share data will build enthusiasm for increased student learning. For agenda topics, college and career target study teams could widen their circle of research and information sharing to include families. Perhaps beginning with a pie chart graph about the percentage of students taking either the SAT or ACT would open dialogue about how the school is encouraging a college and career-going culture and how families can partner in these efforts. Hosting data-informed, interactive, and food-filled events around school data is welcoming and energizing for principals, teachers, and families alike.

GUIDE TO ACTION

Data-friendly Lunch and Learn programs are popular with busy working families. Local businesses are eager to sponsor the casual, family events. Principals, teacher teams, and student groups can highlight learning activities along with participation and progress data. Families can join the conversation about ways to make improvements. School leaders can share digital tools to encourage families to stay connected and watch for more progress.

Family Curriculum Adoption Workshops

Families need to be involved in the *what* of learning so they better understand data and assessment components. School leaders should invite families to review new curriculum adoption products and their accompanying formative assessments. How frustrating it can be when children bring home quizzes or tests over books and materials that families have never seen. Instead, what if family members had opportunities to interact with curricular materials, right when they were adopted, so that families could better support their children at home? Textbook companies have family-friendly print and digital components for extending learning, and all families need access to these opportunities. Learning more about the curriculum and the aligned formative assessment products will help families anticipate what student reports will be available and accessible from school and from home.

REFLECTION QUESTIONS

At a faculty meeting, principals and teachers can reflect upon assessment experiences that impacted their lives in positive ways. School leaders should pose the question: Can you discuss one final exam, test, writing assessment, or performance assessment in high school or college that helped you grow? Sharing specific examples and reinforcing the message that assessments are part of learning will drive greater school improvement.

How do school leaders promote connections among curriculum, instruction, and assessment (CIA) during the school year? In grade-level or departmental groups, teachers can share ideas about how they plan lessons to ensure tight alignment of curriculum and instruction work with useful assessment data. Having a CIA investigation at monthly faculty meetings can be a fun and simple way to ensure that the school remains focused on connecting assessment results with classroom learning.

How do teachers use quick data in their classrooms? Perhaps one teacher would volunteer her classroom as a learning laboratory and model how to collect different kinds of easily accessible data. Then, collaborative conversations could take place about what worked and what did not, leading to richer dialogue about how collecting quick data in day-to-day teaching can contribute to a more accurate diagnosis of learning.

School leaders need to seek feedback from students about innovative ways to celebrate improved student performance and growth. Students will likely have many ideas about ways to recognize peers for not only earning the A grades but also for recognizing academic achievement that requires increased effort. Promoting growth mindsets within a variety of student accomplishments will nurture a culture of continual learning.

Principals and teachers could invite families to reflect on data around a schoolwide initiative. For instance, school and family teams could analyze science assessment data prior to selecting an after school enrichment program. How do student needs identified from data on state and classroom assessments match with criteria in the proposed science enrichment program? Families can then more clearly see how data use strengthens curricular decision-making.

LEADERSHIP TAKE-AWAYS

School leaders should use the Data Work Conceptualization Model to organize data and assessment tasks at the beginning of the year. So many times principals and teachers allow data tasks to overwhelm them when they could easily categorize data and use them to leverage improvement. When school leaders show others a way to conceptualize what data are needed and why, others see the big picture and are eager to join the data work team.

Giving proof of data wins is a tremendous motivator for principals and teachers. Serving as a demonstration site for other school leaders in the district and state can help staff members solidify their Collaborative Data Protocol and share their strong data practices. Having peer visits with the sole purpose of data sharing will also enable principals and teachers to learn about and replicate other successful practices.

Peer observations are powerful professional development tools. Teachers take the lead in selecting topics that they would like to learn more about from peers. For instance, a group of teachers may want to watch a colleague assess higher order thinking skills using a classroom response system. Sharing lessons learned at faculty or grade level meetings strengthens a culture of inquiry.

Student leadership councils enable students to provide input about schoolwide issues. What if school leaders focused one of these sessions on guiding students to develop self-assessment tools to track reading or writing yearlong progress across all subjects in the school? What a tremendous opportunity for school leaders to listen to students about what they are learning and how they think they can best measure their own progress.

How many times do families ask at conferences . . . what can I do to help my child at home? A fresh idea would be for teachers, families, and students to develop data-driven individual modules for extended learning opportunities. Beginning with student data, the group can examine curricular materials and put together an action plan to extend student learning at home.

References

Bangert-Drowns, R., Kulik, J., & Kulik, C. (1991). Effects of frequent classroom testing. *The Journal of Educational Research*, 85(2), 89–99. Retrieved from http://www.jstor.org/stable/27540459

Black, P., & Wiliam, D. (1998). Inside the black box: Raising standards through classroom assessment. *The Phi Delta Kappan*, 80(2), 139–148. Retrieved from http://www.jstor.org/stable/20439383

Darling-Hammond, L. (2014). Assessments for deeper learning: What's next and what will they cost? *The State Education Standard*. March 2014. pp. 32–36. Retrieved from https://edpolicy.stanford.edu/publications/pubs/1228

Every Student Succeeds Act (ESSA, 2015). Pub. L. No. 114–95, 114 Stat. 1177 (2015).

Guskey, T.R. (Ed.). (2009). *The principal as assessment leader*. Bloomington, IN: Solution Tree Press.

Marzano, R.J., Warrick, P., & Simms, J.A., with D. Livingston, P. Livingston, F. Pleis, T. Heflebower, J.K. Hoegh, & S. Magana (2014). *A handbook for high reliability schools: The next step in school reform*. Bloomington, IN: Marzano Research.

Perlman, C., & Redding, S. (Eds.). (2011). *Handbook on effective implementation of school improvement grants*. Lincoln, IL: Center on Innovation & Improvement. Retrieved from www.centerii.org/handbook/

Popham, W.J. (2016). Standardized tests: Purpose is the point. *Educational Leadership*, 73(7), 44–49.

University of Oregon. (2017). Dynamic Indicators of Basic Early Literacy Skills (DIBELS). Retrieved from https://dibels.uoregon.edu/help/

Prioritize and Simplify Curriculum and Instruction

Simple Strategies

- Focus on What Students Need to Learn
- Practice Evidence-Based Instructional Strategies
- Align Reading and Writing Expectations with College and Career Targets
- Monitor Rigorous Reading across all Content Areas
- Intensify Learning through Writing in all Content Areas

A father of a new kindergartner chattered on and on about his child's unbelievable school leader. I smiled to myself, remembering the principal's experience as a phenomenal classroom teacher. She had distinguished herself as a bright teacher leader who helped direct curriculum and instruction efforts at her school. She had crafted innovative lessons alongside colleagues and passionately sought out instructional strategies to personalize learning for students. She was now transforming the school into a larger classroom focused on teaching and learning. The parent was spot on in perceiving that his child was headed for college, career, and life success.

ESSENTIAL QUESTION

HOW DO SCHOOL LEADERS ENSURE THE HIGHEST QUALITY OF CURRICULUM AND INSTRUCTION?

From day one, this first-time parent is confident that his child's principal is a dynamic teaching and learning leader. A curriculum and instruction enthusiast is easy to recognize! Not every school leader needs to be a specialist, but every school leader must understand how to design and deliver the highest quality curriculum and instruction for all students.

Students, teachers, and families want to know that school leaders are placing their efforts and attention where it counts most ... in all classrooms. School leaders need to join teachers and students whenever possible on the front line, whether observing or instructing or both, but definitely reinforcing the value of daily curriculum and instruction. What are our students learning, each and every day, and how? When school leaders are actively involved in the learning taking place in classrooms, they naturally communicate their commitment for greater student achievement.

RESEARCH TIP

Leadership in Curriculum, Instruction, and Assessment Impacts Student Achievement

Marzano, Waters, and McNulty (2005) examine principal leadership behaviors and correlate responsibilities with student academic achievement. In 23 studies involving 826 schools, researchers find a correlation with student academic achievement when the principal has direct involvement in the design and delivery of curriculum, instruction, and assessment (p. 42). A school leader's involvement in planning and implementing curriculum, instruction, and assessment results in greater student learning gains.

Focus on What Students Need to Learn

With a better understanding of college and career targets and data protocol in hand, school leaders can focus on what students need to learn in all classrooms. The *what* would include the local curriculum, the content or subject matter that students learn on a short-term and long-term basis, both inside and outside of school. There is not enough time to teach everything, and principals and teachers must deliberate the crucial question: What should students learn within their limited time, given the multiple college, career, and life challenges ahead?

RESEARCH TIP

Guaranteed, High Quality Curriculum Leads to High Achievement

Marzano (2003) compares factors that most impact student achievement and ranks a "guaranteed and viable" curriculum, which includes time and chances to learn the curriculum, as most important (pp. 19–20). Marzano urges schools to identify essential content, consider instructional times, organize content into topics and sequences, monitor implementation, and protect learning time (pp. 25–31). Darling-Hammond (2010) points to 40 years of research and concludes that teacher quality and curriculum quality are the school factors that matter most to student achievement (p. 54). Rigorous curriculum and effective instruction lead to more opportunities to learn (p. 57).

What does quality curriculum look like at the local level? Principals and teachers should prioritize essential components in curriculum design.

Components of Local Curriculum

Challenging State Academic Standards

ESSA (2015) requires states to adopt challenging state academic standards in mathematics, reading or language arts, and science. Local curriculum is strongly shaped by the standards that detail what students should know and be able to do at the end of each grade. The standards are organized around core knowledge and skills in each content area. Because ESSA (2015) mandates that standards be aligned to higher education and career and technical education standards, school leaders can design local curriculum using these standards and know that they are setting the academic foundations for students' postsecondary success.

RESEARCH TIP

Articulated Core Knowledge Leads to Deeper Learning

Resnick (2001) emphasizes that, in each subject and grade, content learning must include a core of knowledge, higher level thinking, and application of knowledge (p. 5). The core of knowledge should exist within academic standards and be the foundation for an articulated curriculum of deeper learning (p. 5).

School leaders should emphasize content knowledge within the standards. Most school leaders begin educational careers with a passion for content knowledge, whether in art, music, reading, careers and technical education, mathematics, business, social studies, physical education, or science. When school leaders prioritize knowledge, skills, and abilities in all content areas, they expand excitement for learning schoolwide. Extending knowledge is vitalizing and a strong lever for overall school improvement.

Easy Ways to Highlight Content Knowledge

- Have students share ways that content knowledge is connected to future aspirations.
- Have students design animated content trailers (like book trailers) for all subject areas.
- Capture intriguing aspects of content knowledge and display in high-traffic areas.
- Feature career connections with content areas on the school website.
- Encourage teachers to join content-based learning communities.
- Open faculty meetings with a quick focus on different content standards.
- Purchase content-focused journals for staff development activities.

GUIDE TO ACTION

Rotating faculty and parent meetings among different departments and classrooms highlights content learning. All teachers can host meetings in their instructional spaces and spotlight data, curriculum, and best practices. What an easy professional development strategy that bolsters curriculum pride!

STORIES FROM EDUCATORS MAKING A DIFFERENCE EACH DAY

How do school leaders respond when a parent seeks more challenging math work because her child is bored? Do we simply move the student to a higher grade level math class? In some instances, this may be an effective solution, but many times, enhancing the rigor of the math curriculum horizontally is the better option. One middle school teacher is a master at using grade level standards to accelerate students' math skills and abilities. He seamlessly integrates problem solving throughout the math curriculum to give students a context for learning as they apply higher levels of math ideas. Using grade level standards, he poses well-chosen multistep problems that allow students to investigate more difficult math concepts and make natural connections among math tasks. The teacher orchestrates "what if" questions that invite students to struggle as they stretch critical thinking and reasoning abilities. Also, his students build procedural fluency and accuracy through games and competitions so they can access even more complex concepts. In this high-intensity, standards-based classroom, the word *bored* does not exist.

Textbooks

Written by experts and aligned to standards, textbooks (and eTextbooks) provide a logical scope and sequence of essential concepts and topics within content areas. Textbooks make links among topics as curriculum spirals and returns to concepts and skills to reinforce learning. Embedded audio and video tools provide immediate ways to kick up engagement levels and to scaffold support. Ideas for differentiation and enrichment activities enable teachers to immediately adjust content learning to better meet student needs. Big picture themes and cross-curricular connections extend learning across the school.

Textbooks allow students to anticipate learning with text features such as a table of contents, index, glossary, sidebars, headings, margin guides, timelines, pictures, captions, maps, graphs, and bold words. Within eTextbooks, hyperlinks help students access layers of information.

As textbook features become more predictable, students can more readily expend efforts on learning concepts and skills.

Supplementary Materials

Supplementary materials, aligned to textbooks, allow students to continue to make linkages among concepts and skills and heighten learning. Supplementary materials are wise investments to support students at all levels of learning. Print and digital resources offer students multiple exposures to content and more chances to process information. Students read, write, think, and converse about content which leads to deeper learning.

Examples of Supplementary Materials

Mini-lessons	Listening libraries
Primary source documents	Homework extensions
Anthologies	Teaching charts
Consumable workbooks	Unit PowerPoints
Skill builder kits	Vocabulary flashcards
Thematic text sets	Center activities

Online Resources

Student online workspaces provide digital versions of textbooks and supplementary materials. The workspaces give teachers and students more active learning resources, such as, games, adaptive learning programs, and communication and progress monitoring tools. Additional eBooks offer students reading practice and more content learning.

School leaders should be well-versed in the online features of textbook programs to accelerate student and family engagement. Then, in incremental bites throughout the year, school leaders can convey specific ways that students and families can best use the resources. To illustrate, families can help their children in reinforcing daily content learning or in previewing upcoming topics. Instead of having to read ahead and prepare to explain difficult material, families can simply enjoy watching online tutorials about challenging content alongside their children.

Likewise, teacher online workspaces allow anytime access to textbooks and supplementary materials. Teachers can plan ways to heighten students' content learning with easy research and database tools. Helpful features might include unit and lesson planners, communication tools, and ways to customize assessments and track class progress.

Pacing Guides

Pacing guides are indispensable, long-range planning tools. Principals and teachers collaboratively develop pacing guides for consistent implementation of local curriculum across classrooms and schools. Pacing guides provide designated time frameworks for planned sequences of instruction. To illustrate, teachers can simply list the weeks in the school calendar and then align elements within the local curriculum. State standards, units and lessons, curricular resources, major projects, and assessments can be listed on pacing guides.

Using pacing guides gives principals, teachers, and families the reassurance that all students will have chances to learn local curriculum, which is especially crucial for highly mobile students and families. Students frequently move from school to school when dividing time in different households. Having pacing guides will improve the likelihood that, when students move within a district, they will receive the same scope and sequence of curricular opportunities as peers in more stable home and school environments.

STORIES FROM EDUCATORS MAKING A DIFFERENCE EACH DAY

It was 8:00 a.m. on a Saturday morning, and I had anticipated the global language conference session to be rather subdued. Instead, a young teacher welcomed us, sporting a brightly colored scarf with an equally vibrant demeanor. Bursting with enthusiasm and pride, she shared her state's world language content standards and her work with the district's pacing guide. She invited attendees to take a gallery walk around the room which was plastered with samples of her students' diverse learning projects. She offered access to her digital gallery walk with even more active learning ideas. What interested me most was how she used her pacing guide to plan and build momentum for developing the authentic, project-based activities. The teacher was able to weave content learning and creativity throughout the units and lessons that led to students' deeper learning. The 8:00 a.m. session was exhilarating!

Unit and Lesson Plans

With pacing guides in place, school leaders should structure time for colleagues to engage in grade level and subject level curricular work. Designing unit plans together is a productive yet often overlooked professional development opportunity. When teachers develop unit plans in isolation, school leaders and other teachers miss meaningful chances to dialogue about students' content development and engagement during instruction. Ground level unit development adds rigor to learning as many voices determine what content is essential to learning and why. Collaboration generates excitement for building better unit plans and fosters confidence in teachers' abilities to create their own high quality curriculum.

Quick Considerations for Unit Development

- Pacing guides and state standards guide unit development.
- A big picture concept or theme frames the unit plan.
- An essential question focuses the learning.
- Specific objectives measure knowledge and skills that students need to achieve.
- Specific objectives measure noncognitive abilities that students need to develop.
- Students have multiple exposures to main concepts and topics.
- Instructional activities engage students in learning content.
- Differentiation activities support all learners.
- Instructional practices extend learning at school and at home.
- Interventions target needs of low-performing students.
- Ongoing formative assessments monitor student learning.

From unit plans, teachers then craft daily and weekly lessons. Principals and teachers can work in grade level teams to pool collective knowledge and generate robust lesson plans for classroom activities.

Simple Checks for Lesson Development

- ☐ Does the objective specify what knowledge and skills students need to develop?
- ☐ Does prior learning provide the foundation for the lesson?
- ☐ Are ways suggested to strengthen noncognitive abilities?
- ☐ Are key terms or vocabulary words introduced to scaffold learning?
- ☐ Are lesson components explicitly taught and modeled?

☐ Do strategies engage students during guided practice?

☐ Do instructional activities offer students chances for independent practice?

☐ Do differentiated learning activities support all learners?

☐ Will formative feedback guide further learning?

☐ Do activities extend learning at school and at home?

Lesson planning requires teachers to bring the right mix of curriculum, instruction, and assessment for students. Teachers adjust lessons frequently according to observations and student feedback. Also, teachers customize lessons for student groupings, use of technology tools, and availability of supplementary materials. Teachers also consider student issues such as attention span, learning style preferences, and personal interests.

School leaders must reinforce the message that daily lessons are for the students. As school leaders visit classrooms, they should see student-friendly objectives posted conspicuously. Is it clear what students should know and be able to do at the end of today's lesson? Students should be able to talk about what they are learning and how the objectives are meaningful to them.

Practice Evidence-Based Instructional Strategies

How many times have you watched a beginning teacher struggle with student discipline, but upon closer inspection, realize that instruction, not discipline, is the actual problem? Oftentimes, new teachers are handed textbooks and lesson plan books but are given little direction about classroom instruction. They begin the school year frustrated with themselves and their students when clear instructional routines and effective go-to strategies would have made all the difference.

Instructional Routines

School leaders must know and communicate the components of good teaching. Hunter's (1989) well-known model provides a framework for instructional decision-making. Hunter advocates for elements of planning (goal setting, content selection, learning strategies, research), modeling, guided practice, checking for understanding, and independent practice (1989, pp. 16–18). She urges teachers to be flexible and use their own artistry in adapting elements to their particular students (1989, p. 16).

RESEARCH TIP

Instructional Routines Advance Opportunities to Learn

Archer and Hughes (2011) document the importance of explicit instruction in giving all students, especially disadvantaged students, chances to learn new knowledge and skills (p. 17). Archer and Hughes advocate a clear, three-part format for an explicit lesson. The opening grabs the students' attention, explains lesson goals and relevance, and reviews skills (2011, p. 44). The body of the lesson includes modeling and guided practice while the closing includes review, preview, and independent practice (2011, pp. 45–47).

School leaders are likely familiar with simplified instructional routines that move from teacher-led instruction to guided practice to student independent practice. Instructional routines enable students to anticipate the sequence of learning activities which allows them to spend more time interacting with the lesson content. Learning moves at a quicker pace from teacher direction to student independence due to predictability and clear expectations.

Simple Instructional Routine

- Introduction of Content or Topic
- (I Do) Teacher
- (We Do) Teacher and Students
- (You Do) Students
- Check for Understanding

School leaders should promote simple instructional routines that can be easily adapted and implemented across content areas. The following illustrates the application of the simple instructional routine in a middle school language arts classroom.

Application of a Simple Instructional Routine

Grammar Lesson about Pronoun Case Errors—Grade 6

Introduction of Content or Topic
(Attention and Purpose)

The teacher holds up a cell phone and mimics ringing. (Dancing to ring tones adds humor.) She asks students: Do I answer by saying, "This is she," or "This is her"? Turn to your partner and talk: Which pronoun is correct and why?

(I Do) Teacher
(Explicit Teaching and Demonstrating)

The teacher projects a Pronoun Case Chart to help students classify pronoun cases and break down content into smaller segments. The teacher illustrates examples of the different pronoun cases using real life scenarios. The visual scaffold enhances comprehension and memory of pronoun cases.

(We Do) Teacher and Students
(Guided Practice and Support)

The teacher and students practice using pronouns correctly in sentences. The teacher seeks early feedback about pronoun knowledge through response tools such as index cards, dry-erase boards, or digital devices. If students are quick, confident, and correct with responses, the teacher knows she can proceed. If students respond reluctantly or incorrectly, she may need to continue questioning to determine lesson difficulty and furnish additional scaffolds.

(You Do) Students
(Self-directed Practice)

The teacher withdraws supports and provides students with hands-on center activities to practice using correct pronoun cases on their own.

As she circulates and notices problems, she quickly teaches mini-lessons to strengthen particular skills.

Check for Understanding

The teacher elicits responses from small groups and individual students as she monitors understanding and provides immediate corrections.

School leaders who advocate for instructional routines are advocating for student growth. Students become confident learners when they can see definite pathways to growth. When first introducing routines, teachers should be explicit as they explain the procedures from one stage to the next. Students know that new knowledge and skills are explained at the beginning of the lesson, and, then, that they can count on teacher assistance as they practice different strategies. Also, students understand that they will eventually be responsible for applying the knowledge and skills on their own.

Evidence-Based Strategies

Studying research findings is the first step in determining instructional strategies for classroom applications. Students need access to those evidence-based strategies that have the greatest potential to bring about gains in their achievement. Good teaching involves having an arsenal of effective practices that can be applied throughout all stages of instructional routines.

With research in hand, principals and teachers are ready to consider which strategies will be effective for different content areas, for designated learning activities, and for specific students. How can various evidence-based strategies intensify learning throughout the stages of instructional routines, for instance, during whole group, small group, and individual work tasks? Collaborating together and spelling out what makes high quality teaching and learning is crucial to growing a learning culture. Veteran teachers can share how to make the connections between evidence-based strategy selections and the wide range of student needs. The sky is the limit for the variety and creativity that principals and teachers can bring to routines with a rich mix of effective strategies.

RESEARCH TIP

Elements of Good Teaching Improve Achievement

Marzano (2007) finds elements associated with improved student achievement. As examples, Marzano documents the need to establish clear goals, to track progress with frequent formative assessments, and to recognize success in knowledge gains (pp. 9–15). Having students chart their performances on assessments allows them to clearly see gains toward goals (pp. 25–26). Other research highlights effective strategies in specific areas. For instance, Marzano and Simms (2014) present evidence-based strategies around higher-order and lower-order questioning. Magaña and Marzano (2014) offer over 100 evidence-based strategies using technology integration that improve student learning.

Flexible Strategies to Use in Instructional Routines

Graphic Organizers align with the lesson's purpose and scaffold learning to help students see relationships among ideas. Types include: cause/effect, compare/contrast, fact and opinion, flow chart, problem/solution chart, time order, Venn diagram, t-chart, and word web.

Annotation builds active readers who think, make connections, and self-question. Students see a logical flow to learning as they jot notes in margins, highlight main ideas, circle key words, and draw arrows to show connections. Students can annotate before reading (make predictions), during reading (find similarities and differences), and after reading (summarize and synthesize).

Read Alouds enable students to access complex text. Teachers read texts aloud first, engaging students in conversations while making links among key ideas, new vocabulary, and text language. Students enhance background knowledge and gain self-assurance prior to reading difficult text.

Video Snippets add graphics and sound to seize students' attention. Bite-size segments of content shown before a lesson stimulate excitement. Snippets shown during a lesson add intensity, and snippets shown after a lesson help students process content in deeper ways.

Socratic Seminars allow students to listen more intently to multiple view-points and expand thinking. After students have read about a topic, teachers model purposeful questioning, and then students continue the questioning to spark discussion and drive more learning.

STORIES FROM EDUCATORS MAKING A DIFFERENCE EACH DAY

Sometimes, beginning teachers just do not know about instructional strategies available to them. As a fourth year teacher, I signed up for the state's career ladder program where an evaluation team visited classrooms unannounced. I admit that, at this stage in my career, I signed on for the money! The four evaluators came on a good day. My lesson plan was polished; I moved through well-paced activities, and transitions were spot-on. In the post-conference, the evaluators began by praising my planning, procedures, and push for rigor with inner city students. Then they glanced at each other, and I knew that look. They politely acknowledged that I did not establish any relevance to prior learning. They suggested I try "shop talk" where students chat for 2–3 minutes to ignite personal connections. I thought to myself that I would definitely lose control if I encouraged talking at the beginning of class. Later, when I tried it, the instructional strategy worked. Students began to talk in purposeful ways and to connect to lessons more quickly. If not for the evaluators, my inner city students would have missed important chances to engage with others in learning.

Principals and teachers should have data-based conversations about which strategies will be consistently reinforced across the school. Given our students' learning needs, what two or three practices should be the school's signature strategies? What two or three practices will students know well so that they can use seamlessly in combination with other effective strategies? To illustrate, students can use flexible strategies like outlining and notetaking across all curricular areas. By consistently applying strategies schoolwide, students have multiple and varied opportunities to practice and make strategies their own.

Student Engagement

ESSA (2015) draws fresh attention to the engagement of students in their learning. ESSA stipulates that not less than one indicator of school quality or student success needs to highlight meaningful differentiation in school performance and includes options for these indicators (2015). Listed first among the options are student engagement and educator engagement (ESSA, 2015).

RESEARCH TIP

Engagement Strategies Improve Learning

Marzano, Pickering, and Heflebower (2011) find categories of strategies for daily use that promote high engagement: effective pacing, intensity and enthusiasm, positive teacher-student and peer relationships, and verbal feedback (pp. 147–149). Jensen (2013) focuses on how engagement strategies can raise student achievement, especially for economically disadvantaged students. To illustrate, helping students develop context and meaning for learning builds deeper understanding (p. 101). Jensen suggests telling stories, teaching vocabulary, using writing tasks, sharing visuals, and employing drama as ways to boost engagement (pp. 101–106).

How come that in some classrooms . . . high engagement is simply the norm? Lessons move at an energizing pace, and students and teachers engage in activities with intensity. However, as easy as some teachers make it appear, student engagement does not just happen. Effective teachers continuously seek out evidence and experiences from colleagues and refine their collections of go-to engagement ideas and strategies. Then, teachers plan, and then plan some more, to ensure that all students connect with learning opportunities. As lessons progress, teachers continue to read students' engagement levels and readjust strategies.

Simple Ideas to Skyrocket Engagement

- Immerse students quickly in doable bell ringer activities.
- Keep a purposeful flow to lessons.
- Model interest in learning with lesson artifacts.
- Use storytelling to enliven learning.
- Create energy with flexible instructional groupings.
- Use interactive or manipulative curricular materials.
- Interject wordplay to enhance vocabulary.
- Experiment with dramatic re-enactments.
- Reframe content focus to add relevancy.
- Bring enthusiasm to all lesson components.
- Empower students with different technology tools.
- Add humor unexpectedly to lesson segments.
- Give frequent feedback during lessons.
- Invite students' speculation about upcoming topics.

STORIES FROM EDUCATORS MAKING A DIFFERENCE EACH DAY

The room was quiet and close to bell time in an inner city classroom. I was observing a class that had spent several days probing character development in *The Red Badge of Courage*. Students had just finished role playing different characters to experience their perspectives. Today, they were rotating through learning stations in order to make character profiles, write imaginary resumes, and conduct character interviews. A student named LaTonya asked if she could share a comment. She said she really enjoyed this English class because the time passed so quickly. She added that students in this class were not discipline problems. I know the teacher was touched with the gratifying comment more than winning any award. Having a teenager praise bell to bell engagement in front of peers was certainly an accolade for effective teachers everywhere!

Align Reading and Writing Expectations with College and Career Targets

Curriculum and instruction leaders should be prepared to help students find success on the college and career targets ahead. What can be very frustrating to students, teachers, and families alike is hearing about higher expectations and not understanding their connections to K-12 curriculum and instruction. And, what is equally disheartening, given the multiple and formidable challenges, is not perceiving the likenesses among the targets themselves.

Table 3.1 expands the college and career targets to include reading and writing expectations. School leaders can use Table 3.1 to show students and families the clear connections among the college and career targets and the needed literacy skills. The visual assists school leaders in confirming the importance of higher levels of reading and writing knowledge and skills to students' postsecondary success.

Never before has it been as essential for students to be accomplished readers and writers. To help prepare students, principals and teachers must look closer at the alignment of the literacy expectations among the targets. For instance, what reading and writing skills and abilities do students need to master challenging state academic standards versus what reading and writing skills and abilities do students need to be successful on the SAT and ACT? What do college-level reading skills and abilities look like in Advanced Placement courses compared with reading and writing skills and abilities necessary for students to be successful in career and technical courses?

GUIDE TO ACTION

Connecting K-12 teachers with college faculty can lead to a fuller understanding of postsecondary reading and writing expectations. Offering teachers chances to visit college campuses (and college faculty to visit K-12 classrooms) will open communication lines about needed skills and abilities. From observations and reflections with college faculty, principals and teachers can better prepare students for the literacy demands ahead.

How can principals and teachers use knowledge about reading and writing similarities among the targets to strengthen local curriculum in all content areas?

Table 3.1

College and Career Targets and Reading and Writing Expectations	
Challenging State Academic Standards	• Reading standards aligned to college coursework and career and technical education standards • Writing standards aligned to college coursework and career and technical education standards • Literacy standards across content areas
High School Graduation Requirements	• Required courses with reading and writing expectations • Literacy standards across content areas
High School Transcript	• Reading and writing courses at challenging levels • Grades showing evidence of high reading and writing achievement
High School Exit Exam	• Mastery of challenging state reading standards • Mastery of challenging state writing standards
Advanced Placement Courses and Exams	• College-level reading skills and abilities • College-level writing skills and abilities
Dual Credit Courses	• College-level reading skills and abilities • College-level writing skills and abilities
SAT and ACT College Admissions Tests	• College-readiness reading skills and abilities • College-readiness writing skills and abilities
Career and Technical Education	• Rigorous reading across all content areas • Rigorous writing across all content areas

Monitor Rigorous Reading across all Content Areas

The significance of reading achievement on college and career targets presents new opportunities. Through a few bold actions, school leaders can make a big impact. The data protocol will be the school leader's best tool to refocus and drive the most pressing reading achievement needs for all students. Schoolwide improvement will be reenergized with new learning in teaching reading across content areas.

Close Reading, Text Evidence, and Complex Text

What exactly is the make-up of reading achievement in higher college and career level contexts? Major shifts in reading expectations are illustrated within the College and Career Readiness (CCR) Anchor Standards for Reading (NGA Center & CCSSO, 2010). CCR Reading Standard 1 requires students to "*Read closely* to determine what the text says explicitly and to make logical inferences from it; cite specific *textual evidence* when writing or speaking to support conclusions drawn from the text" (NGA Center & CCSSO, 2010, p. 10). CCR Reading Standard 10 requires students to "Read and comprehend *complex literary and informational texts* independently and proficiently" (NGA Center & CCSSO, 2010, p. 10). The words and phrases add multiple dimensions to K-12 student reading achievement.

Reading closely for details, analyzing *text evidence*, and reading *complex texts* independently are not new. However, these practices have been intensified in the language within the standards. Students must look deeper within a piece of challenging text, valuing evidence as opposed to seeking personal connections and reactions. Students must learn to use evidence within a text to support ideas and conclusions. Students must navigate text structures that add meaning and recognize elements of the author's language. Students must read and re-read passages for different purposes. Most importantly, students must develop the stamina needed to read complex passages independently.

RESEARCH TIP

Evidence-Based Strategies Improve Reading Achievement

Researchers document elements that are critical to improving adolescent reading achievement (Biancarosa & Snow, 2004). Examples of the elements include explicit instruction in comprehension, collaboration around multiple texts, use of diverse texts at varying difficulty levels, and continuous formative assessment (pp. 13–20). Researchers advocate for a combination of the right elements that best meet student needs (p. 12).

What does evidence-based reading instruction look like in classrooms? First of all, teachers are reading aloud short, quality passages, asking students to follow along and look for a different purpose than from a prior read. Students are processing thinking as they make text-to-text connections using various graphic organizers. Collaborative discussions are taking place in whole and small groups with students going back into the text to talk about words and phrases that led them to their answers. Students are using multiple documents to interpret evidence across texts. After rich post-reading discussions, students are deepening conceptual understanding by writing in journals or posting to class blogs.

GUIDE TO ACTION

Growing reading teachers is as important as growing students' reading achievement. School leaders should locate professional resources about evidence-based reading strategies and encourage teachers across content areas to lead workshops. *Reading Next: A Vision for Action and Research in Middle and High School Literacy* is one such free resource that builds in-house experts (Biancarosa & Snow, 2004).

Wide Reading

As evident from an in-depth look at the college and career targets, not only will students need to read closely but they will also have to read widely and independently. Achieving high levels of reading comprehension equates to much effort and many hours of practice. School leaders must aggressively seek out wide reading opportunities that push students to make significant reading growth.

RESEARCH TIP

Students Need Time and Opportunities to Read

Allington (2001) emphasizes the strong relationship between reading volume or the time spent reading and students' reading achievement (p. 33). Research shows that, in comparison with less effective teachers, more effective teachers offered students at least twice as much material to read in social studies and science content areas (p. 34). Biancarosa and Snow (2004) confirm that other reading strategies will not bring about improvement if students do not have enough time to practice (p. 20).

The more students read . . . the better readers they become . . . and the more they learn. Students need to read independently within the complex texts used in classroom instruction as well as to read widely during and outside the school day to build reading fluency and stamina. Students must experience an extensive range of genres and topics within literature and informational texts, such as literary nonfiction and historical, scientific, and technical texts. It is important to expose students to many authentic reading sources. What fun for teachers and students to try French recipes, explore bird types using field guides, or read technical manuals and repair household items together.

STORIES FROM EDUCATORS MAKING A DIFFERENCE EACH DAY

One image of my students experiencing wide reading remains vivid. At a private academy nestled among bayous, adolescent girls sit under elm trees, immersed in reading *A Separate Peace*. The girls lean against each other's backs in a familiar fashion, periodically reflecting on the meaning of the whole text. The girls are vicariously experiencing another time period and culture, which prompts informal conversations about themes of rebellion versus conformity, innocence versus corruption, and conscience versus guilt. Testing out their ideas immediately as they read alongside peers inspires them to consider other perspectives and develop a fuller interpretation of the literature. Reading the whole text with the encouragement to look deeper into layers of meaning nourishes a habit of lifetime inquiry. The girls are self-directed critical readers and thinkers ready for the global world.

Easy Ways to Elevate Wide Reading

Model reading as a pleasurable activity outside the classroom. School leaders with books in hand in hallways and at after school functions show their commitment to reading and have ready dialogue to engage students and families.

- Ask media specialists to ramp up outreach programs. Giving students more choices in outside reading will be motivating for them as they take on greater text length and strengthen their reading fluency.

- Encourage class or grade level reading competitions during holidays. A quick check can take place when students return, and the highest achieving class earns a celebration. Choosing books of different topics and genres will introduce students to more sophisticated vocabulary and broaden reading interests.

- Partner with the local library to bring more student and family reading programs into the school.

- Connect online with authors to allow students to hear how authors create characters, themes, and plots. Students will see writers as real people, which will give them confidence in their own abilities to grow as readers and writers.

- Take schoolwide walks with parent organization members and examine classroom libraries. Do all classrooms contain texts of quality and substance to enable students to build reading stamina? Do class collections span all reading levels? Challenge the organization to augment classroom needs.

- Invite local businesses to donate vouchers so that low income students can make purchases at reading fairs.

- Host an after school faculty book club that reads, chats, and laughs together.

Schoolwide Reading Analysis

Armed with a data protocol, school leaders are reading champions, ready to ensure that all students have chances to grow as readers. School leaders must first look at student reading progress on multiple measures. Principals and teachers can use the Schoolwide Reading Analysis Questions to examine reading progress on state, schoolwide, and classroom assessments (eResource C). What actions can teachers take to make short and long term improvements in student reading progress? What do item analyses reveal about specific skills and abilities that can help teachers intervene with more targeted reading support?

Principals and teachers can also use the Schoolwide Reading Analysis Questions to investigate and assess the quality and quantity of student reading activities (eResource C). Building reading rigor involves looking at the teaching of reading across all subject areas with a greater scrutiny of students' in-class and outside reading opportunities.

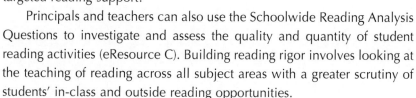

STORIES FROM EDUCATORS MAKING A DIFFERENCE EACH DAY

It took me about five years as a teacher to realize that you could get much more out of students when you gave them options. To promote wide reading, the media specialist and I selected an assortment of novels of varying reading levels, and then she joined the class to pique interest about themes and plots. Students could select from the large assortment of novels, and most made choices matched to their reading levels. One reluctant reader, Taylor, did select the shortest novel, Hemingway's *The Old Man and the Sea*, because his grandfather used to take him fishing. Students read the novels on their own schedules with a deadline for the final essay. Taylor got a C+ on the assignment, largely because he missed the deadline, but in his essay, he acknowledged that this was the only outside book that he read in high school.

Intensify Learning through Writing in all Content Areas

Just as greater reading achievement equates to increased opportunities on college and career targets, greater writing achievement, too, leads to students' postsecondary success. School leaders must look more intentionally at writing expectations across targets and build in opportunities for students to strengthen those skills and abilities. Using writing as a lever for improvement efforts will not only help students move closer toward college and career targets, but it will also intensify learning across all content areas.

Text Types and Purposes

Across college and career targets, the writing spotlight is on *text types and purposes*. School leaders will want to study the expected writing outcomes. From career and technical education to higher levels of academic standards, students must focus on writing types that have closer connections to real audiences and real purposes. Principals and teachers must ask: What kinds of writing tasks will employers expect of students? What kinds of writing assignments will college faculty require of students? And, what kinds of writing proficiencies will students need to engage as responsible citizens?

Argumentative Writing

The College and Career Readiness (CCR) Anchor Standards for Writing define specific types and purposes expected of students (NGA Center & CCSSO, 2010, p. 18). CCR Writing Standard 1 requires students to "Write *arguments* to support claims in an analysis of substantive topics or texts, using valid reasoning and relevant and sufficient evidence" (NGA Center & CCSSO, 2010, p. 18). The higher levels of state standards are focused on evidence-based writing or writing to sources. Instead of writing personal reflections, students write about the texts in front of them.

To educate students and families about the higher expectations, school leaders should dissect CCR Writing Standard 1. Words and phrases to highlight include "arguments," "claims," "analysis," "substantive topics or texts," "valid reasoning," and "relevant and sufficient evidence" (NGA Center & CCSSO, 2010, p. 18). School leaders should focus on the meaning of each word to students' writing development. Do we want our students to be effective communicators, capable of supporting their claims with strong reasoning? Having conversations about why students need argumentative writing will be helpful.

Classrooms where *argumentative writing* flourishes are busy places! After completing database searches to acquire information on multiple perspectives, students are sorting through facts, figures, details, quotations, and other sources of data that they have collected. Teachers are thinking aloud to help students analyze evidence in logical ways. Students are beginning outlines to organize information, listing logical reasons for their positions yet acknowledging claims from opposing views. Later, they will hone oral language skills, defending positions to peers using objective language, and then weigh the validity of others' claims. Students will align research with one side, formulate an argument with credible sources, and connect logical reasons in well-organized essays.

GUIDE TO ACTION

To fully understand the challenging writing targets, families need to experience *writing to sources*. After projecting a chart of kinds of evidence, such as data, survey results, and quotes, school leaders should provide families with samples of informational text. School leaders can pose questions and urge families to locate evidence to support their responses. Using intriguing samples of informational text adds play to the task!

Informative/explanatory Writing

CCR Writing Standard 2 requires students to "Write *informative/explanatory* texts to examine and convey complex ideas and information clearly and accurately through the effective selection, organization, and analysis of content" (NGA Center & CCSSO, 2010, p. 18). School leaders need to break down the *informative/explanatory* writing type into smaller parts. "Convey complex ideas," "clearly and accurately," and "analysis of content" display the general writing purpose of increasing knowledge about topics. In most instances, students will have background knowledge about topics, and they will add to that knowledge with new primary and secondary sources of information. The informative/explanatory writing type helps students learn more in order to explain ideas and procedures to others. In the workplace or higher education, students must gather information and produce memos, manuals, reports, summaries, and critical analyses.

STORIES FROM EDUCATORS MAKING A DIFFERENCE EACH DAY

The College Board honored an Advanced Placement (AP) Psychology teacher with exceptionally high student participation and exam scores. The achievement was impressive as the teacher encouraged numerous students to take AP Psychology, even those performing at average levels in other courses. However, not until my own child had AP Psychology was I fully able to understand the teacher's craft. My teenage son would arrive home and immediately begin psychology homework while other texts remained closed. For AP Psychology my son had a single yellow folder with his name printed neatly across the top. Inside were teacher-created, writing outlines to help students break down the higher levels of psychology content into manageable chunks. I looked at the outlines in amazement, wondering how much time had gone into their creation. The teacher constructed an outline frame of the day's lesson and then provided spaces for students to extend learning through informative/explanatory writing about the complex ideas and critical content. The outline frames assisted students in bridging the gap from teacher-directed learning to independent learning. Through the well-planned approach, students were making powerful linkages among reading, writing, and higher-level thinking. The teacher's ability to connect writing to learning is a best-kept secret for AP success.

Narrative Writing

In CCR Writing Standard 3, students will "write *narratives* to develop real or imagined experiences or events using effective technique, well-chosen details, and well-structured event sequences" (NGA Center & CCSSO, 2010, p. 18). Narrative writing increases in sophistication through grades as students develop experiences or events with dialogue, details, and descriptions. To more closely explain this writing type, school leaders should initiate conversations about the reasons for narrative writing. In the workplace, students must write about organizational processes, report information, reply to questions, and relay information in past, present, and future points of views.

RESEARCH TIP

CCSS Writing Standards Have Strengths and Opportunities

Troia and Olinghouse (2013) find that the Common Core State Standards (CCSS) strongly support writing practices such as prewriting/planning/drafting, text structure instruction, and peer collaboration (pp. 349–351). Other practices, such as, process writing, strategy instruction, setting product goals, and utilizing rubrics, are not strongly promoted by the CCSS (pp. 349–351).

The Writing Process

To be prepared for challenging writing expectations in college, careers, and life, students need comprehensive instruction. Writing is a process, and students need access to all stages of writing development. Like the need for students to practice reading, students also need frequent and varied chances to explore and practice writing.

RESEARCH TIP

Students Need Right Mix of Writing Strategies

Graham and Perin (2007) identify evidence-based elements that improve writing of adolescents. Examples of the elements include writing strategies, summarization, collaborative writing, and study of models (pp. 11–21). Researchers advocate a combination of practices that are most effective with certain students (p. 12).

Students need to be instructed in evidence-based elements of the writing process. School leaders must make writing instruction a priority within school improvement efforts. Teachers need time to share expertise and experiences about a rich mix of effective practices that will increase writing growth for all students.

Quick and Effective Writing Strategies

Brainstorming—Nothing can take the place of teachers and students beginning the writing task as a class, generating a free flow of ideas that stimulate even more ideas. Prewriting strategies, like brainstorming, ensure a solid start to writing and increase student motivation and confidence.

Looking at Writing Exemplars—Students need to see exemplars early in the writing process. Putting a weaker paper side by side with a stronger paper helps students see the criteria that determine quality work. Comparing one element at a time, such as style, is helpful.

Addressing Key Errors—Having a laser-like focus on writing errors will go a long way to improving writing achievement. Teachers observe students' patterns of mistakes during the writing process and adjust instruction immediately. Students can see that their incremental changes in writing result in significant improvements.

Conferencing—Listening to students individually gives teachers an exact point in which to introduce needed skills. Asking students open-ended questions about ways to improve their writing enables them to reflect and take ownership of their learning.

Peer-Editing with Checklists—Peers should edit writing tasks together using pre-established and well-understood criteria. During the peer revision process, students benefit from receiving constructive, non-graded feedback.

Publishing—Students need opportunities to produce numerous pieces of writing for different purposes and audiences. Students will push themselves harder to produce quality writing when they have real audiences, especially their own peers.

GUIDE TO ACTION

School leaders should see students thinking and writing together. Providing one tablet device for small groups forces students to acquire information and integrate new knowledge efficiently. Analyzing complex ideas and writing together will foster persistence and ready students for teamwork tasks in the workforce.

Schoolwide Writing Analysis

Using the data protocol, school leaders should track writing performance and growth on state, schoolwide, and classroom assessments. What trends are apparent in student progress on specific writing standards, and how can adjustments be made on pacing guides to strengthen identified aspects of writing development? What are the key errors that students are making, and how can all teachers help address the errors? For instance, if students at one grade level are performing poorly on writing conventions, teachers across all subject areas in that grade level could adopt the same editing checklist. Or, if students at one grade level are performing poorly on writing organization, teachers across all subject areas in that grade level could teach prewriting strategies to help students generate and better structure ideas before they begin writing. School leaders can use the Schoolwide Writing Analysis Questions to lead Inquiry and robust conversations about writing progress (eResource D).

School leaders should also use the Schoolwide Writing Analysis Questions to examine the quantity and quality of student writing (eResource D). The tool will assist school leaders in assessing students' opportunities to practice the higher levels of writing types. How many opportunities do students have to complete substantial writing products? How many chances do students have to experience the various stages of the writing process (planning, drafting, revising, and editing)?

Easy Ways to Add Writing to Daily Lessons

- Open today's lesson with a vocabulary word from a prior lesson. Have students jot down two to three sentences to predict how this word will connect with learning in today's lesson.

- Capture interest quickly by projecting a photo of new content. Ask students to write about what they know already.

- Read a chunk of content from complex text. Pose a debatable question. Have students work in pairs to write short scripts featuring opposing views.

- Build critical thinking and writing fluency by asking students to discuss difficult concepts with a partner and then write about the thoughts of the partner.

- Share a chart with statistics from the day's lesson. Have students describe the purpose and meaning of the chart in their own words.

- Ask students to summarize the day's lesson in a few sentences. Teachers can learn much from students' candid written feedback.

 STORIES FROM EDUCATORS MAKING A DIFFERENCE EACH DAY

After the Thanksgiving holiday, I announced to my students who were repeating Senior English that they would complete a portfolio assessment instead of a final exam. Students would carefully review their major writing products and assess their growth over the semester. They would compile portfolios of their best writing products to take home as holiday gifts to families. They were required to revise and include a character sketch of a family member. Although I overheard at least one "I can't believe this ###," students began to work in groups to seek feedback about strengths and weaknesses in their writing. The student-directed learning led to greater insights about what determines quality writing. And, as students revised family character sketches, they shared memories and laughed together. On the day that students were to take the portfolios home, I arrived with bags of ribbon and festive paper, and, with holiday music playing, they wrapped their portfolios together. At that point, I began to believe in holiday magic.

Reading-rich classrooms must also become writing-rich classrooms. The level of urgency is great as students must read and write for different purposes and for various audiences, important skills needed as students move into higher education and the workplace. How exciting for students to become better readers, writers, researchers, collaborators, and thinkers! And, who better to champion that charge than school leaders, the top curriculum and instruction advocates for students!

REFLECTION QUESTIONS

School leaders need to consider their own content connections. What content area captured your interest and lured you into teaching? In your leadership role, are you keeping current with your content specialty? What extra efforts are you making to nurture content learning schoolwide?

School leaders should reflect upon the teaching strengths that they bring to the school. Are others aware of your willingness and abilities to model certain instructional strategies? How are you reaching out to students and teachers to share instruction expertise?

Within your collaborative data protocol, how are you using formative assessments to track reading and writing progress? How are you communicating students' progress of reading and writing skills to families? And, how are you educating students and families about the urgency for students to develop higher levels of reading and writing skills?

As school leaders conduct classroom walkthroughs, they can reflect upon students' reading experiences. Are students developing the reading stamina needed for college and career success? How are teachers working to promote quantity and quality of reading experiences for all students?

College and career level writing includes argumentative, informative/explanatory, and narrative types. Do students have enough chances to experience all three writing types? What school improvement work is needed to ensure that all students have access to challenging writing opportunities?

LEADERSHIP TAKE-AWAYS

ESSA's requirement that states adopt challenging academic standards has promoted widespread resource creation (2015). Many state departments of education offer curricula matched to higher levels of standards, and many products are free and easily accessible. School leaders should devote professional learning time to enable teachers to browse and collaborate around curriculum development on the different state department of education websites.

By talking with teachers ahead of time, school leaders can then join classrooms and introduce daily lessons. School leaders can help students restate learning goals in crystal-clear ways. Or, to increase engagement levels, school leaders can introduce thought-provoking excerpts to preview new content.

School leaders should ask teachers to respond to sample ACT or SAT writing prompts. Then, using rubrics from posted guides, teachers should score their own responses. What key errors did the group make as a whole? Teachers can talk together about how they can better structure lessons that prepare students for the greater reading and writing challenges ahead.

School leaders need to be equipped with one or two reading comprehension strategies that they can model at any grade level and in any content area. How exciting for the principal to join classes, share a brief video, and facilitate roundtable discussions! Students will look forward to having school leaders contribute to classroom learning with different ideas and methods.

Sharing effect sizes of writing strategies adds the evidence-based piece to school improvement work. School leaders can jumpstart writing improvement with research (Graham and Perin, 2007) and collaboration about classroom applications. Healthy discussions about evidence-based practices build more competent writers.

References

Allington, R.L. (2001). *What really matters for struggling readers: Designing research-based programs*. New York: Longman.

Archer, A.L., & Hughes, C.A. (2011). *Explicit instruction: Effective and efficient teaching*. New York: Guilford Press.

Biancarosa, G., & Snow, C.E. (2004). *Reading next—A vision for action and research in middle and high school literacy: A report to Carnegie Corporation of New York* (2nd ed.). Washington, DC: Alliance for Excellent Education.

Darling-Hammond, L. (2010). *The flat world and education: How America's commitment to equity will determine our future*. New York: Teachers College Press.

Every Student Succeeds Act (ESSA, 2015). Pub. L. No. 114–95, 114 Stat. 1177 (2015).

Graham, S., & Perin, D. (2007). *Writing next: Effective strategies to improve writing of adolescents in middle and high schools—A report to Carnegie Corporation of New York*. Washington, DC: Alliance for Excellent Education.

Hunter, M. (1989). Madeline Hunter in the English classroom. *The English Journal*, 78(5), 16–18. doi: 10.2307/819193

Jensen, E. (2013). *Engaging students with poverty in mind: Practical strategies for raising achievement*. Alexandria, VA: ASCD.

Magaña, S., & Marzano, R.J. (2014). *Enhancing the art & science of teaching with technology*. Bloomington, IN: Marzano Research Laboratory.

Marzano, R.J. (2003). *What works in schools: Translating research into action*. Alexandria. VA: ASCD.

Marzano, R.J. (2007). *The art and science of teaching: A comprehensive framework for effective instruction*. Alexandria, VA: ASCD.

Marzano, R.J., Pickering, D.J., (with Heflebower, T.) (2011). *The highly engaged classroom.* Bloomington, IN: Marzano Research.

Marzano, R.J., & Simms, J.A. (2014). *Questioning sequences in the classroom.* Bloomington, IN: Marzano Research Laboratory.

Marzano, R.J., Waters, T., & McNulty, B.A. (2005). *School leadership that works: From research to results.* Alexandria, VA: ASCD.

National Governors Association Center for Best Practices & Council of Chief State School Officers. (2010). Common core state standards for English language arts & literacy in history/social studies, science, and technical subjects. Washington, DC: Authors. Retrieved from http://www.corestandards.org/ela-literacy

Resnick, L.B. (2001). Making America smarter: The real goal of school reform. In A.L. Costa (Ed.), *Developing minds: A resource book for teaching thinking* (pp. 3–6). Alexandria, VA: ASCD.

Troia, G.A., & Olinghouse, N.G. (2013). The Common Core State Standards and evidence-based educational practices: The case of writing. *School Psychology Review*, 42(3), 343–357. Retrieved from naspjournals.org/loi/spsr

Strengthen Learning with Relationship Building

Simple Strategies

■ Strengthen Student Capacity through Differentiated Learning

■ Boost Student Capacity with Classroom Teams

■ Enhance Principal and Teacher Capacity through Modeling and Coaching

■ Expand Principal and Teacher Capacity with School Improvement Rounds

■ Forge Meaningful Family Partnerships

In traveling to five large urban districts to study leadership and student achievement, I gained a richer perspective about what was working and why. School leaders graciously shared state test scores, formative assessment results, and classroom intervention charts, and we talked over coffee about strengths and opportunities. We toured classrooms and schools, and principals and teachers brought their student achievement data to life. In a Chicago school, the principal excitedly described ways he was working with leaders of student clubs to broaden participation. In Boston, teachers packed a hotel conference room to learn more from a renowned expert about reading strategies. In New York City, the principal and teachers, clad in shorts and t-shirts, were rooting through boxes to find high-interest materials for summer programs. In Washington D.C., teacher leaders and the students' grandparents were making interactive learning activities to engage students at home. When I had corresponded with the district about my study, certain school leaders were recommended, and I saw why. School leaders joined in with students, collaborated with staff, connected with families, and were moving student achievement forward with clarity and ease. My "aha moment" came when I realized that while it appeared effortless, these leaders pursued a multitude of relationships to take learning to the next levels. Relationship building was a well-calculated component of their teaching and learning plans.

ESSENTIAL QUESTION

HOW DO SCHOOL LEADERS BUILD CAPACITY FOR TEACHING AND LEARNING AMONG STUDENTS, TEACHERS, AND FAMILIES?

These urban school leaders were not highly regarded for undertaking costly initiatives or singlehandedly managing arduous projects. However, upon closer observation, it was clear that their students were growing achievement in phenomenal ways. During conversations, the school leaders were quick to point out that connections among people mattered. School leaders had the know-how and the passion to leverage powerful relationships to accelerate teaching and learning.

These principals had the right combinations of school purpose, quality curriculum, instruction, and assessment, and intentional relationships to bring about greater student learning.

School Purpose

    + Quality Curriculum, Instruction, and Assessment

        + Intentional Relationships

           = Greater Student Learning

Figure 4.1 Simple Capacity Building Formula

Implementing a capacity building formula begins at the top. As urban leaders walked confidently from floor to floor, they relayed specifics about schoolwide goals, curriculum, instruction, assessment, and special programs. As they encountered students, teachers, and families, school leaders chatted in prideful ways about the work of others and commented on productive, collegial relationships. The school leaders had meaningful ties to people and programs. A shared language existed about how the principal, teachers, students, and families needed to pull together to help students confront the postsecondary and workforce challenges ahead.

ESSA (2015) advances the significance of relationship building for greater student performance and for enhanced teacher development. Relationship building helps the school increase capacity to provide the comprehensive and differentiated support needed by students. Also, teachers will serve in new leadership roles and connect with colleagues in productive new ways. For instance, ESSA recognizes the need for teachers to move into leadership pathways such as instructional coaching, mentoring, and school improvement facilitators. Taking ESSA's lead, school leaders should seek out fresh and robust ways to strengthen those relationships among students, teachers, and families that accelerate learning.

Strengthen Student Capacity through Differentiated Learning

School leaders who put student development first make capacity building look easy. Accelerating student capacity begins in classrooms in the midst of good teaching and learning. As principals and teachers work to move students closer to college, career, and life goals, they must first guarantee that daily classroom instruction is of the highest quality and meets all students' needs. How are we structuring classrooms in order to make sure that each student is making maximum growth? What kinds of supports are in place to meet the needs of individual students? Building student capacity must not include fragmented components but instead be a continuous process of principals and teachers making the right student-focused connections.

RESEARCH TIP

Classroom Differentiation Strengthens Student Capacity

Tomlinson and Imbeau (2010) claim that differentiation involves continuous thinking and reflecting about how to vary learning within high-quality classrooms (p. 13). Principals and teachers should modify content, process, product, and affect to meet the readiness, interests, and learning profiles of individual students (2010, pp. 15–18). In differentiated classrooms, teachers are responsible for helping all students find ways to learn important curriculum (2010, p. 14).

With a strong local curriculum and solid instructional routines in place, teachers can more carefully consider students' individual learning needs. Varying backgrounds, different skills and abilities, cultures, language proficiencies, interests, and motivational levels contribute to each student's learning every day. Differentiated instruction is a way to match the learning needs of each student with the necessary supports for optimal learning. To help students reach ambitious goals, teachers must capitalize on students' diverse strengths, draw from a wealth of strategies and resources, and find ways to personalize learning. To build student capacity, school leaders must grow an improved culture of learning, one student at a time.

Curricular Adaptations

School leaders should initiate conversations around textbooks and supplementary materials and their differentiation components. How are our curricular materials giving all students more chances to learn? Vendors have invested much research in product development to allow all students to gain access to content and deeper learning skills. Within teachers' editions, sidebars contain guidance about ways to meet multiple student needs, such as for English Learners, special education students, and high ability students. Textbook vendors frequently offer differentiated content training. The core text materials are a simple place to start, and then a wealth of teacher-generated ideas and materials can add another valuable layer for differentiating content.

GUIDE TO ACTION

Special education, gifted/talented, and English Learner teachers are just waiting to be tapped to share evidence-based ways to differentiate instruction. These teachers have received extensive training that is woefully underutilized. Having specialized professionals present techniques about how to adjust curriculum, instruction, and assessment to meet student needs will strengthen the school's common language of good teaching. Discussion boards can generate even more ideas and enthusiasm for modifying classroom practices.

Connecting local curriculum to students' interests and aspirations powers up learning. When students choose to engage with content, the more likely they are to remember and make meaning from that content. Teachers know their students' preferences and can bring curricular resources that match interests to abilities and skills. For instance, if students are studying world geography, teachers can bring in role playing scripts with rich cultural dialogue. Sharing captivating primary and secondary sources tied to concepts of world geography adds depth to student background knowledge. Travel brochures written at varying levels provide colorful descriptions and graphics to boost content connections. When teachers link students' strengths and choices with essential content, students are much more motivated to learn. Students will develop deeper learning skills, such as thinking critically and communicating effectively, when they are meaningfully engaged with content.

Digital environments ratchet up students' interest levels and help match content to student learning preferences. Content with graphics, images, pictures, diagrams, and video provides support to visual learners. Music, stories, and other multimedia tools help auditory learners. Kinesthetic learners benefit from games, simulations, and hands-on, interactive apps.

Modified Learning Process

Well-planned, ongoing formative assessment informs instruction in differentiated classrooms to ensure that all students' needs are being met. With formative assessments, teachers continuously assess student readiness for lesson tasks. Which students need more targeted support and on what specific skills? What practices will be most effective in helping students access new knowledge and skills? Using benchmark data, teachers can then gauge where during instructional routines to modify the learning process and provide necessary supports. Students respond to individual attention from teachers and connect their immediate feedback to learning. Personalized feedback promotes caring relationships between teachers and students and furthers students' motivation for more learning.

Differentiated learning takes place during all stages of instructional routines. Teachers have multiple windows during explicit teaching, guided practice, and individual study to vary learning for students. As school leaders observe instructional routines, they will notice learning processes that change quickly and intentionally based on teachers' ongoing thinking about student needs.

Easy Ways to Differentiate Learning during Instructional Routines

I Do
(Building Background Knowledge)

In differentiated classrooms, teachers explicitly prepare students for new learning. Teachers conduct whole-group brainstorming sessions to help students with metacognition, or thinking about their thinking. Students can then better connect prior knowledge to new ideas, concepts, and vocabulary. Together, teachers and students can complete graphic organizers about what content they know and about what content they want to learn to bolster readiness for more learning.

We Do
(Questioning)

Teachers ask varying levels of questions to differentiate learning for specific students. With the right questions, teachers maximize participation and build student confidence. Students will benefit as teachers link student ideas to expand learning to higher levels. Teachers also stretch learning with more questioning about similarities and differences among topics. Students become more active in questioning themselves, leading to more independent learning.

You Do
(Flexible Grouping)

Teachers group and regroup students consistently based on multiple factors such as lesson content, student abilities, and assessment results. To illustrate, teachers may want to cluster groups around progress toward completion of tasks so that teacher support can more effectively target students furthest behind. For example, when completing projects, some students will be in the final stages, ready to work in significant ways with peers. Other students may still be struggling with organization and need more explicit instruction with mini-lessons or teacher think alouds.

Check for Understanding

Students can respond to open-ended questions. What progress did you make today toward the lesson objective? What else would you like to learn?

Varied Learning Products

Students need multiple ways of demonstrating their learning. How can teachers design culminating learning tasks that address the readiness, interests, and learning profiles of all students (Tomlinson & Imbeau, 2010, pp. 15–18)? When working with a large classroom of students, designing varied learning outcomes may sound overwhelming, but several ready formats simplify the process.

Multi-Level Groups and Tasks

To differentiate product formats, teachers begin by grouping students with tasks and curricular materials at varying levels of complexity. Teachers use the same objectives and lesson content but adjust learning products to account for students' readiness levels and the knowledge and skills that they need to develop. For instance, all students explore the same social studies content and engage in learning activities together. However, due to her pre-assessment of student skills and abilities, the teacher varies the groups' critical thinking expectations within the end-of-unit performance tasks.

Learning Contracts

Individualized contracts give students more control over learning. Choice within contracts motivates students to explore topics based on interests, aspirations, and abilities. Students and teachers conference about product goals and jointly create written guidelines of expectations. Adjustments are made within work tasks to give students more practice where needed. Adding a peer reflection component helps students process information, promotes self-discovery, and leads to ownership of learning.

Performance Products

Students self-select from a menu of performance products. Students can work individually, in pairs, or in small groups, pending topic interests and diverse skill sets. As evidence of learning, students produce preferred products, such as infomercials, re-enactments, demonstrations, or plays, and stretch their capabilities as active learners. Well-established rubrics, given ahead of time, clarify expectations for quality work.

Technology Products

A multimedia environment quickly opens up student product options. Teachers can connect students to real world applications and new performance modes. For example, students can assume roles of animated docents who provide audio tours or podcasts into family historical backgrounds. Students use mobile devices to interview and hone speaking and listening skills. Technology adds a substantial dimension to personalize learning as students search, blog, and tweet in the creation of online products.

Teachers need to consider students' levels of independence as they design product formats for students. Some students will have appropriate maturity levels to work at their own paces and navigate well the freedom that accompanies open-ended tasks. Other students will lack maturity and need further teacher clarification of tasks and more structure in the pacing of their work.

GUIDE TO ACTION

Principals and teachers can talk about preferences in their own learning products. If given the choice to demonstrate your knowledge and skills, would you select a multiple choice test, an essay, a hands-on project, a digital portfolio, an oral presentation, or something else? How can we integrate more types of learning products and performance modes into our units and lessons? How can we better match learning products with students' strengths and preferences?

All students deserve to understand strengths and opportunities in their learning. Principals and teachers should honor diverse learning preferences and create inviting environments that recognize and value all levels of growth. School leaders need to build cultures where teachers continuously think about ways to focus on what students can do and support students in developing capacity for more learning. Differentiated learning builds academic rigor by supporting students as they gradually move along the learning continuum toward independence. When students witness their own growth and take ownership of learning, they will be armed with confidence and motivation to aspire to higher challenges.

Boost Student Capacity with Classroom Teams

Cultivating strong teams within classrooms elevates student capacity. Athletic coaches are well-known for inspirational locker room speeches about the importance of players working together. The coach sends the unmistakable message that the group's success in overcoming obstacles depends on teamwork. In classrooms, too, teachers must champion the same message. Students must work together in groups, supporting and pushing each other forward toward higher goals.

The bar has been raised, and the need for principals and teachers to construct classroom teams has never been greater. Standards are higher, and employers want employees who can reason well, think critically, and work collaboratively. K-12 classrooms must be places where students can engage in the higher levels of learning needed through increased inter-activity and productivity in team building activities.

STORIES FROM EDUCATORS MAKING A DIFFERENCE EACH DAY

As a young teacher, I wanted the principal to observe my classroom. I was enthusiastic about trying different ways for students to work together, and I wanted his feedback. Maybe after spending long hours on lesson plans . . . I even wanted to brag a bit. I left a note in his mailbox, welcoming him to come anytime, and he arrived during fifth period, definitely the most spirited group. My classroom teams were immersed in collage projects, using buttons, yarn, wallpaper, fabric, and glitter, and interacting with symbolism in unique ways. Students were building academic rigor, remixing the author's intent with their own innovative renditions. As the principal walked past one team, one girl exclaimed shrilly, "##!!%, that's wicked good!" I ignored the comment, making the choice to correct her language later rather than interrupt team dynamics (also noting silently "there went MY evaluation"). However, later, when I encountered the principal in the hallway, he grinned and commented, "I was simply amazed at watching Jillian. She has missed so many days this year, and it was heartwarming to watch her connect with the group." That school leader GOT IT and inspired me to take more risks in designing classroom teams.

Effective teachers grow student capacity purposefully through design of classroom teams. These are the teachers who, besides knowing their teaching craft well, know their students equally well and recognize the importance of meeting students' academic, social, and behavioral needs simultaneously. These teachers care about students and go deeper to shape student relationships in authentic ways, resulting in more productive and healthy classrooms.

Purposeful Classroom Teams

Learning Teams

Students are arranged in a variety of learning teams frequently to complete tasks and grow from collective learning. Grouping students of all academic abilities encourages some students to stretch thinking and others to consider ideas from different angles. As an example, after art teachers provide instruction about how to achieve unity through patterns and color, students can then work in smaller groups to apply the new knowledge. Creating an assemblage together allows for ideas to expand and multiply as students vary shapes and colors, explore concepts in depth, and discover more learning.

Media Teams

Students become journalists in all content areas. For instance, groups of students investigate details about upcoming local events, tied to local curriculum, and produce feature stories. To be prepared for future careers, students need to experience real audiences and authentic situations. Contributing with peers in meaningful ways toward mutual goals yields greater motivation and better quality productions.

Corner Conversation Teams

Even in crowded classrooms, corner conversation teams are ready forums for students to process thinking. Movement brings new energy to academic tasks as teachers ask students to quickly move to assigned corners of the room. Tasks are already posted, leaving room for sticky note responses. Ground rules clarify expected outcomes. Mixing students frequently adds different voices and cultural perspectives to conversations.

Debate Teams

Students become passionate about content learning when they conduct research, develop a cohesive viewpoint, and become accountable to each other for the group's success. Students interact around substantive topics and strengthen critical thinking skills. Debates link classroom content to real-world issues, causing students to persist in defense of viewpoints and become involved citizens.

Quality Teams

In quality teams, students think in more calculated ways about growing their work in the midst of production. For instance, in any content area, students can examine multiple models and rank them in order by quality characteristics. Together, students analyze the models and annotate why certain ones are exemplars. Students learn to pay attention to techniques and details so that they can emulate elements of the exemplars in their own work. The focus on excellence extends better work habits into other learning arenas.

Literary Analysis Groups

Using varying levels of texts by the same author gives all students access to higher levels of thinking and literary analysis. Teachers and students collaborate to select the text match for each student, based upon interests, reading abilities, and motivation. After reading their chosen texts independently, students come together to analyze differences and similarities among plots, characters, and themes in the varying texts. Students at all ability levels contribute to group dynamics and are exposed to rigorous learning.

School leaders should structure professional learning around creating purposeful classroom teams. Teachers who are successful at creating classroom teams can lead roundtable discussions at faculty meetings. Having dialogue around noncognitive factors that students are developing will motivate colleagues to try new formats. Principals and teachers will want to rethink classroom designs for the more frequent student interactions. Desks, chairs, and tables should be arranged to facilitate the different kinds of learning that principals and teachers want to take place among students. Likewise, mobile devices encourage movement, create new spaces, and expand the potential for more classroom teams.

Enhance Principal and Teacher Capacity through Modeling and Coaching

Building greater student capacity requires boosting principal and teacher capacity! Teaching is complex, and principals and teachers must pool talents and abilities and accomplish more together than they can alone. Growing adult capacity through professional relationships is a strategic investment for greater student development.

RESEARCH TIP

Capacity-Building Improves Adult and Student Learning

Fullan (2014) emphasizes that school leaders should devote energies to capacity-building. School leaders should build professional capital, a combination of human capital, social capital, and decisional capital, to improve adult and student learning (pp. 67–71, Hargreaves & Fullan, 2012). Fullan stresses that it is still important to develop individuals, but learning alongside teachers in groups accelerates impact (2014, p. 55).

Modeling and Coaching

No longer are traditional workshops and webinars the only and most effective ways for principals and teachers to gain additional knowledge and skills. Instead, experimenting with professional growth designs opens up possibilities for greater impact. On the ground level, principals and teachers have the most accurate data, know their students' needs, and offer the best chances of crafting their own learning that connects to greater student performance and growth.

School leaders must weave proven practices into the school day to strengthen adult learning. Principals and teachers invest much time in studying professional materials to understand the *what* of evidence-based practices. Modeling and coaching, however, take learning to the next level with application of *how*.

When teachers model and coach together, they affirm the efficacy of various teaching practices. Teachers use modeling for demonstrating techniques and coaching for observing and providing feedback. However, many schools also use a combination or blending of the purposes of modeling and coaching. Modeling and coaching formats are molded to address identified professional needs, teacher preferences, and available resources. Modeling and coaching enable teachers to work alongside colleagues in more personalized ways, demonstrating, collaborating, and creating better practices together. Modeling and coaching partnerships can be highly structured or more loosely defined. Simply, modeling and coaching improves the quality of teacher learning that results in better student learning.

RESEARCH TIP

Coaching Improves Collaboration and Professional Learning

Joyce and Showers (2002) conclude that when schools build structured professional development forums such as coaching, they are on a path of improvement (p. 89). Coaching leads to multiple benefits such as a common teaching language, group lesson planning, and collaborative problem-solving (pp. 88–90). Knight (2011) adds that effective coaching involves partnership principles, such as reciprocity, where partners simultaneously teach and learn (p. 20). Knight advocates for partnerships where teachers learn and question together, collaborate about best teaching practices, and interpret data together (p. 22).

Adult learning must be a well-coordinated part of teaching and learning in order to improve student outcomes and impact school culture. Use of the Data Work Conceptualization Model (Figure 2.1) sharpens thinking around the school's comprehensive data and the professional development roles needed to drive the data work. Using rich data alongside a clear plan for professional learning leads to greater motivation and commitment. How can principals and teachers grow more relationships to push students closer to higher levels of learning? How can modeling and coaching facilitate more adult and student learning? The model's components of school improvement, professional development, classroom instruction, and student performance and growth provide a systematic way to grow meaningful adult roles.

Modeling and Coaching Roles

School Improvement

Modeling and coaching powers up school improvement work by involving principals and teachers in multiple leadership roles. School teams oversee schoolwide organizational improvement and reaffirm a shared belief in high student expectations. Teachers serve as facilitators and coaches for school goals and objectives implementation, schoolwide strategy use, and data analysis around state, district, and school assessments.

Professional Development

Teachers serve as models and coaches in thinking more purposefully about teaching attitudes, behaviors, and desired student results. Models and coaches act, observe, and provide feedback to each other as they apply various strategies during instructional routines. For example, colleagues work alongside each other in trying inquiry-based learning methods. Which approaches are yielding the best outcomes? Teachers advance their own professional competence and institutionalize the school's belief in teacher-driven learning.

STORIES FROM EDUCATORS MAKING A DIFFERENCE EACH DAY

Even with little formal training, modeling and coaching can absolutely work! Being tasked rather spontaneously to co-teach with a colleague in a remedial English class resulted in significant professional learning.

Our personality styles were never analyzed for compatibility, and we had no e-learning modules about the effective stages of coaching. Instead, a colleague and I were simply paired together to lower the class ratio for struggling students. Very quickly and out of necessity, we simply became models and coaches for each other. That first day, I began our lessons by plunging into literary terms and the historical context behind the reading. Within ten minutes, several heads went down. Then, more heads went down. Fortunately, my colleague began moving around the room, scaffolding support with verbal prompts and cues. Using humor, he gave vocabulary words new life. His individual questioning connected students' background knowledge to challenging content. And, my colleague's amusing anecdotes reduced complex themes to understandable ones. When I saw evidence of the success he was having with students, I adopted different practices myself. I modified routines to add interest and student choice. I strengthened lessons by appealing to students' learning styles. And, I tried more "kid watching" formative assessments. In reflecting, we did experience modeling and coaching elements of shared expectations, willingness to learn, and respect and trust for one another. While he may have gained a fuller appreciation of literary terms, my take-away was a much clearer understanding of the differentiated behaviors I needed to adopt to help all students succeed.

RESEARCH TIP

Teacher Relationships Matter to Student Achievement

Leana (2011) finds that the social capital of teachers was a greater predictor of student achievement increases than teacher ability or classroom experience (p. 33). When teachers had both high ability and strong social capital, students made the greatest math achievement gains (pp. 33–34).

Classroom Instruction

Teachers power up classroom instruction by observing, asking questions, demonstrating, and re-directing students together. Teachers study their craft as collaborative peers, considering evidence and making contextual applications with different students. Teachers coach each other to experiment with new practices and technology tools. Colleagues are hands-on, co-learners in more mindfully connecting adult performances to student learning.

Quick Modeling and Coaching Reflection Questions

- What teacher behaviors helped students meet today's lesson objective?
- How did teachers monitor lesson flow throughout the instructional routine?
- How did teachers use evidence-based strategies to improve learning?
- What teacher supports were most useful to students?
- How did teachers use feedback to make lesson adjustments?

Teachers need chances to build learning relationships with peers. How exhilarating to provide teachers with meaningful opportunities during the day to share classroom expertise! Perhaps one teacher is especially adept at helping students think critically and could coach others in questioning methods. Perhaps another teacher has flawless transitions within instructional routines that she could demonstrate for colleagues. School leaders who leverage "right there" classroom expertise are making smart investments in professional growth.

Student Performance and Growth

When principals and teachers model and coach together, students have greater access to optimal learning. Principals and teachers drill down into classroom evidence and reflect together about ways to scaffold learning. What are we learning from data, and how can we link our knowledge to better practices to help students learn? Do we understand how to ask the right questions to collect the data we need to most effectively help students?

Collaborating around student work adds rigor to the learning as teachers coach each other in designing rubrics and other self-assessment tools.

Logistics of Modeling and Coaching

A teaching and learning school is always on and involves everyone. School leaders must be forward thinkers about professional growth—relentlessly advocating for and communicating their beliefs In the power of collaborative learning. Naysayers will claim that teachers should not leave their classrooms to model and coach elsewhere. However, one hour of quality school-based learning may equate to several weeks of inspirational teaching that engages many more students.

Principals and teachers who want to make modeling and coaching happen during the school day will problem solve and find solutions.

Easy Ways to Schedule Modeling and Coaching

- Modeling and coaching can be scheduled during open periods of a substitute teacher.
- Parents can volunteer to conduct demonstrations and enrichment activities, opening up teacher time for learning.
- Teachers can volunteer individual planning periods, team periods, or department meetings to model and coach with others.
- Community guest speakers may be scheduled for multiple classes, providing windows for modeling and coaching.
- Teacher teams can create larger groups for appropriate activities, providing classroom coverage for colleagues to learn.
- Smaller blocks of time may be slated for modeling and coaching as opposed to full class periods.
- Many teachers will be honored to be "tapped" as coaches for others and will gladly offer time after school to share professional expertise with colleagues.

School leaders who seamlessly weave modeling and coaching into teaching and learning increase the rigor of professional dialogue and offer professionals a sense of personal inclusion. Principals and teachers need to work together through trial and error to determine what types of embedded modeling and coaching structures are most effective for their schools. Modeling and coaching builds more instructional leaders, enhances teaching practices, fosters trust, and improves school culture.

Expand Principal and Teacher Capacity with School Improvement Rounds

Observing medical rounds at a comprehensive cancer center makes anyone a believer in the power of networking and knowledge sharing among professionals in improving outcomes. It was memorable to witness this capacity-building protocol firsthand and observe how attending physicians, residents, and medical students entered rooms and conducted collaborative, patient-centered discussions. Differing opinions of residents and medical students were welcomed by attending physicians. Watching a team of professionals share intelligence, energy, and concern for patients was truly inspirational. How fortunate for physicians, residents, and medical students to have such high quality professional learning embedded so consistently and seamlessly into daily routines.

School leaders should use the highly respected medical model to build more capacity for leadership and learning in schools. The power of the medical training model is in its simplicity of collective learning and its alignment with daily practices. City, Elmore, Fiarman, and Teitel (2009) developed a similar approach for teams of educators entitled "instructional rounds" (p. 3). The researchers define the rounds process as "identifying a problem of practice, observing, debriefing, and focusing on the next level of work" (City et al., 2009, p. 6). The rounds approach enables educators to build relationships and more learning as they grow a common language and culture and reduce teacher isolation (City et al., 2009, p. 10).

School leaders have the exciting opportunity to look closely at the components of medical rounds and select those that work best in their school settings. Just as students need differentiation in classrooms to build their capacities as learners, principals and teachers, too, need preferred and personalized approaches to strengthen their capacities as learners.

> **RESEARCH TIP**
>
> ## Instructional Rounds Grow Collaborative Cultures
>
> City (2011) advocates that rounds enable peers to form networks of colleagues who meet regularly and grow trusting relationships (p. 38). Likewise, Marzano (2011) states that the learning during rounds is for teachers doing the observing, enabling them to learn from peers, reflect on their own practices, and build collaborative cultures (p. 80). De Luise (2014) adds that medical rounds facilitate learning within complex environments and that educators, too, should benefit from such collaborative and synergistic learning (p. 5).

Similar to modeling and coaching, school-based rounds experiences embed meaningful professional learning into daily teaching and learning. Simply, observing peers, asking questions, and reflecting upon self-improvement is significant adult learning. Principals and teachers should share responsibilities for implementing quality practices and for growing their own learning simultaneously.

School Improvement Rounds

An easy way to begin is to fold the rounds process into continuous school improvement work. School improvement rounds are just one of many variations of rounds that principals and teachers can employ. Principals and teachers will need to review the school purpose, data protocol, and schoolwide strategies and identify the highest priority areas for learning.

In designing rounds, principals and teachers will want to ensure that staff members have opportunities both as individuals and as a collective group to grow professional learning. Principals and teachers should consider: How can participating as a rounds team impact student learning and overall school improvement? What specific components of learning rounds will be most useful to us? And, what kinds of formats can we devise that will provide structure, yet allow flexibility to differentiate our own learning?

Easy Ways to Conduct School Improvement Rounds

- Determine school improvement priority areas for professional learning.
- Write questions to focus the learning.
- Visit classrooms and observe learning conditions around the questions.
- Process thinking about individual and schoolwide learning of observed behaviors and practices.
- Discuss ways to continue more teacher-focused learning experiences.
- Discuss ways to continue more schoolwide learning experiences.
- Reflect upon ways that the schoolwide learning has led to actionable outcomes.

Like growing the Collaborative Data Protocol, designing school improvement rounds from the ground up rallies principals and teachers around the school's purpose and creates buy-in and enthusiasm for learning. Participating in inquiry around one's own and schoolwide practices adds the dimension of relevance which results in greater motivation for more learning. Principals and teachers will consider their own curiosity, expertise, and interest in classroom applications in determining priority areas for observations.

Feedback Logs for School Improvement Rounds

Principals and teachers should develop a consistent way for gathering feedback from the rounds. For teacher and schoolwide learning, observers will want to describe those teacher behaviors and practices that show evidence of classroom impact on student growth. To illustrate, rounds teams can create learning logs to describe what they are observing. When rounds teams begin with observation questions, they organize the learning around inquiry, seeking out the best teaching practices that benefit students. Teams communicate the clear message that they are probing their own assumptions and teaching behaviors as part of professional learning. The open-ended format encourages more extensive responses, allows for personal insights, and leaves room for follow-up questions. As opposed to evaluative or summary comments, writing about actual observations will lead to fuller reflections. School improvement rounds teams can customize logs in accordance with the purposes and tasks of their rounds. The School

Improvement Rounds Learning Log contains sample observation questions (eResource E).

After classroom observations, rounds teams need time to process their thinking together. The rounds team may choose to use a consistent discussion format in which to share and build upon others' observations, or the team may prefer to simply have an open discussion of observations of teacher behaviors and practices around the observation questions. What did we learn about new or alternative practices? Listening and allowing new ideas about quality teacher practices to emerge will power up collaborative reflections. Having opportunities to connect thinking with classroom evidence and data will build communities of reflective learners. Principals and teachers can use the School Improvement Rounds Learning Log to guide classroom observations as well as to facilitate thoughtful debriefing sessions (eResource E).

The rounds team may reflect upon improvements that teachers plan to make in classrooms as well as modifications that the school can make to improve outcomes. What professional learning opportunities will teachers find valuable in implementing aspects of the school improvement plan? And, more specifically, what commonalities have emerged in our reflections about school improvement that can better direct our professional learning? What new learning can we now cycle back into school improvement planning?

Teacher-Focused Learning Rounds

School improvement rounds are easily adapted to more specific areas of teacher need and interest. For instance, if a school improvement plan includes a goal of greater student engagement, principals and teachers may want to narrow the focus of the rounds so that observers think more critically about engagement practices. Observation questions can focus the learning on engagement across all classrooms.

Sample Observation Questions for Student Engagement

- How are teachers creating active and responsive learning environments for students?
- What student–student and what teacher–student activities show evidence of active learning?

- How are teachers nurturing noncognitive abilities to bring about greater student engagement?

- How are teachers increasing student task persistence toward completion of final products?

- What student–student and what teacher–student activities are resulting in deeper learning?

- What types of classroom teams are bringing about maximum student engagement?

GUIDE TO ACTION

School leaders can explore even more learning using the medical model of Grand Rounds. Grand Rounds take place outside patient rooms, usually in a larger arena. More professionals are invited to these forums which offer ways of openly sharing practices with colleagues across departments. Physicians, residents, or medical students present patient cases along with current research and medical opinions. Perhaps school leaders can ask local medical residents to assist in personalizing a Grands Rounds experience for their schools.

School leaders who employ school improvement rounds build more instructional leaders in classrooms and across schools. Professional dialogue becomes more inclusive with diverse voices and more energy. And, school leaders have greater confidence that professional growth aligns closely with school and teacher goals, ultimately translating into better student outcomes.

As rounds teams visit classrooms, they are observing through lenses of self-improvement and school level improvement. Peers interact with the shared purpose of improving teaching and learning, and the school moves closer to a healthy learning culture. Yes, school leaders can begin the rounds process with lengthy agendas, detailed procedures, and documentation requirements. Or, the rounds can be as plain vanilla as principals and teachers observing to gain fresh ideas and think more deeply about their own practices. Or, the rounds can be somewhere in-between! The bottom line is that principals and teachers are sharing instructional leadership responsibilities around the common focus of high quality student learning.

RESEARCH TIP

Building Teacher Capacity Supports Principals

The School Leaders Network (2014) spotlights troubling principal turnover and advocates for building leadership teams to better distribute school improvement and leadership responsibilities (p. 13). Designing teacher teams and empowering teachers spread leadership opportunities and create stronger schools (p. 13).

School leaders want the rounds for their school to emerge and expand in ways that guarantee buy-in and commitment for continual learning. Oftentimes, the easiest way generates the biggest impact!

Forge Meaningful Family Partnerships

Engaging families has never been more critical for student success. School leaders are faced with recalibrating families' expectations about the amount of learning needed for their children to meet college, career, and life goals. Families hear about current unemployment statistics (or experience firsthand), note employment shifts in twenty-first century job types, find out from friends about children not being admitted to colleges, and, of course, discover the realities of exorbitant student loans. Many families are seeking engagement in K-12 schools like never before, largely due to anxiety about their children's futures, while other families remain unaware and disconnected.

GUIDE TO ACTION

School leaders should help families act. The National PTA (www.pta.org) has numerous online resources to empower families in supporting their children. A family section provides parent information about state assessments and higher standards. Free guides contain easy activities for families to extend learning at home.

Family Engagement

Building vibrant family and school partnerships must include strengthening families' understanding about the higher expectations ahead for students. Schools have expertise about the college and career targets, and families want to know about updates and available resources so that they can support their children at home. Having accurate and timely knowledge about information that impacts their children's futures empowers families of all backgrounds. When they are aware of the challenges ahead, families see the big picture and note the incremental steps, such as more practice at home, that will be needed for their children's success. Families have hopes and dreams for their children and want to be a meaningful part of the school/home team. When principals, teachers, and families have the same knowledge base, family and school partnerships become stronger and more credible, and good things happen for students.

RESEARCH TIP

Principals and Teachers Must Engage Families

Epstein et al. (2002) claim that it does not just happen that schools are communicative; instead, principals and teachers must have the know-how to work with families and the community in collaborative and democratic ways (pp. 35–36). Ferlazzo (2011) points to the difference between families being involved and being engaged (p. 12). For better results, school leaders must engage families in reciprocal dialogue and function as partners (p. 12).

STORIES FROM EDUCATORS MAKING A DIFFERENCE EACH DAY

I am reminded of a biology teacher who was passionate about improving family engagement. I was serving as an assistant principal when she commented to me that families seemed to be invited into the high school more for athletic reasons than for academic ones. As we chatted, her students were getting ready to dissect owl pellets, a favorite lab activity. We talked about how much fun it would be to invite families to participate alongside their children. We thought that the lunch hour might be the best time to maximize attendance. We were not sure about how to begin, but I knew we would be okay moving forward with this bright and extremely organized science teacher. We simply acted on the idea—sent out invitations—and had a room bursting with parents and students for the dual dissection project. Due to the teacher's creativity, parents and students laughed together, enjoying firsthand experiences with science inquiry. Interestingly, we had a few students without parents in attendance, but, wordlessly, other families warmly made room for them. I quickly realized that school leaders should reach out more often and invite families to join classroom learning with their children.

Family and School Partnerships

Principals and teachers must seek out different types of engagement venues to bolster partnerships with families. Being engaged early and often goes a long way in building the trust necessary to sustain healthy relationships. Families want to know that principals and teachers are providing the highest-quality education, and they want school leaders who can effectively involve them in ways that improve their children's chances for success. From making home visits to hosting school forums to using social media blasts, family and school communication forums are rapidly expanding and simplifying ways of linking home and school. Constant communication and involvement reinforce the belief that families and schools are allies, all helping to develop in students the knowledge, abilities, and stamina needed to keep on track toward future goals.

School leaders who focus on student and teacher relationship-building must strengthen school and family partnerships with the same gusto! What are those credible ways to engage families in school activities that really matter?

School Improvement Partners

Along with principals, teachers, students, and community members, family members serve as collaborative members of school improvement teams.

Families have significant and shared leadership responsibilities in envisioning purpose, analyzing data, setting goals, and determining schoolwide strategies for student success.

Problem-Solving Partners

Families join specific committees with principals and teachers to seek solutions for pressing schoolwide issues. As examples, families can serve on grading committees, helping principals and teachers consider what academic feedback is most beneficial for school and home use. And, how can student academic feedback be provided in understandable and family-friendly formats?

Student Learning Partners

Families include an interesting and diverse mixture of adults with much to offer to student learning. Families can contribute as experts in multiple content areas. For instance, families can enrich classroom lessons with vibrant artistic and social cultural activities. Or, perhaps family members can model use of emerging technology tools or robotics in the local workforce.

GUIDE TO ACTION

Family members become school partners with jigsaw learning activities. A jigsaw can be as simple as dividing up educational journal articles or blogs and then reporting out in small groups. Meetings take on new life when families have the latest research in hand and assume significant roles as speakers and listeners.

Community Liaison Partners

Family members are inspirational resources to connect what students are learning in classrooms to real world contexts and local communities. Family members can assist principals and teachers in exploring resources that the community has to offer that are aligned to classroom learning.

Vast resources abound within local service clubs, arts organizations, cultural centers, conflict resolution groups, and public libraries. Willing parents can plan, organize, and host community guest visits that expand student access to local resources and enrichment activities.

Career Partners

Students will value opportunities to hear about multiple career paths from real people in the local workforce. And, their connections as family members to their peers will automatically magnify credibility! Family members can share artifacts and information about skills and abilities needed in certain careers, reinforcing relevance and motivation for students' greater learning. Equally important, family members can add anecdotes about how they persevered and overcame obstacles to obtain higher learning or advanced workplace skills. Students will see that growth mindsets are powerful in transforming career goals.

RESEARCH TIP

School Involvement Looks Differently for Some Families

Nieto (2011) shares that her own immigrant parents felt uncomfortable about attending school events and appeared disconnected to her learning (pp. 130–131). Years later, Nieto realized that they were involved in more meaningful ways by reinforcing the need to do homework and to pursue an education (p. 131). Also, O'Sullivan, Chen, and Fish (2014) find that low-income families, regardless of their education, increase their children's mathematics achievement by providing structure in the home for math assignments and practice (pp. 183–184).

School leaders must advocate that all families have important capacities to partner with schools in their children's learning. Educators should recognize and respect varying types of family engagement, and no one way is the only way. Just because parents do not have college educations or industry certifications does not mean that they cannot motivate children to higher learning or be effective in supporting learning at home. School leaders should be the first ones to reassure families that they, themselves, are not content and pedagogy experts in all areas. School leaders should explain that providing structure for homework and practice is just as important, or maybe even more so, than assisting in other ways.

Easy Ways to Bolster Academic Ties with Families

- Leverage skills and abilities of families in classroom projects.
- Host one-day family camps about topics of interest.
- Use social media to blast out practical homework and study tips.
- Include families in extended day, extracurricular events.
- Invite family members to serve as guest speakers.
- Link school and home learning with interactive performance tasks.
- Co-design a family and school toolkit for enrichment in multiple content areas.

GUIDE TO ACTION

Principals and teachers should re-connect with students and families the following year after students leave the school. Families will have valuable feedback about their children's learning and the school's home connection strategies. Perhaps siblings are only a few years away, and school leaders can invite them now to attend the school's academic, athletic, and social events.

Principals and teachers need to embrace all that families have to offer and build relationships that bolster student success. A tenacious school leader with a mobilizing team of teachers and families can do what no single educator or family member can do alone. Ineffective piecemeal efforts will be transformed into something more democratic and much more meaningful.

Together, schools and families can create partnerships of trust and mutual respect that will be sustainable and ongoing for the next generation of learners.

REFLECTION QUESTIONS

What do data within the Collaborative Data Protocol reveal about the needs of students' academic skills and noncognitive factors? How are teachers adjusting curriculum, instruction, and assessment in all content areas to target these needs? When principals and teachers observe classrooms, which differentiation strategies are having the most impact?

By purposefully structuring team-centered classrooms, teachers facilitate improved relationships and learning among students. What kinds of team learning opportunities exist in all classrooms? What feedback do teachers, students, and families provide about the effectiveness of the classroom teams? How can school leaders expand team building across the school?

Students who are reaching for higher targets need principals and teachers who are reaching for higher levels of professional learning. Teachers share that modeling and coaching alongside colleagues is reaffirming, reenergizing, and relevant to their learning. How can school leaders best organize and motivate teachers to either begin or expand modeling and coaching? How can school leaders likewise stretch themselves to model and coach and add to a learning culture?

How can school leaders leverage school improvement rounds for greater professional learning? What kinds of initial dialogue should principals and teachers have to generate interest and enthusiasm for this kind of learning process? Perhaps school leaders can share video clips of hospital rounds and pose questions: What advantages does the model have for adult learning? How could its application strengthen schoolwide and individualized teaching and learning practices?

How can school leaders build relationships with families that result in greater student learning? How can school leaders highlight the successful family engagement activities of individual teachers and scale those up into larger schoolwide efforts?

LEADERSHIP TAKE-AWAYS

In grade level groups, principals and teachers should examine pacing guides, units, and lessons and integrate ways to differentiate learning based upon elements of content, process, and product (Tomlinson & Imbeau, 2010, pp. 13–15). School leaders should tap veterans to lead conversations about how they quickly and intentionally adjust classroom instruction to better meet students' needs.

Classroom teams bring about more student engagement. Having a classroom team talk about their learning at a faculty meeting affirms students' relationship-building and increased learning. Together, principals and teachers should look strategically at pacing guides for opportunities to build in more team-based learning. How can teachers use classroom teams to build meaningful connections, improve engagement, and create more supportive classrooms?

Growing principal and teacher capacity must be a significant component of teaching and learning. Using the Data Work Conceptual Model (Figure 2.1) is an easy way to anchor modeling and coaching and structure relevant professional learning. So many times, schools have pieces of interesting professional development taking place, but schools and students can also suffer from an overload of disparate training parts. Instead, school leaders should seize rich data within the school's own priority areas to drive systematic and relevant modeling and coaching efforts.

Principals and teachers may elect to use school improvement rounds to learn more about the implementation of schoolwide strategies and how they can work toward self-improvement. As an example, principals and teachers can create observation questions around close reading implementation. What would we like to learn about different close reading approaches and their impacts on student learning? Rounds provide teachers with tremendous opportunities to learn more about close reading applications and reflect on ways to improve both collectively and individually.

How can principals and teachers foster greater family and school connections? As part of school improvement, principals, teachers, and families should include goals to ensure that families are meaningful partners in their children's learning. Action plans can further outline specific activities to engage families as motivators and facilitators of learning at home.

Perhaps capacity building becomes a goal with the inclusion of activities that foster trusting and open relationships between families and schools. Broadening thinking to ways different from our own is a wonderful beginning!

References

City, E.A. (2011). Learning from instructional rounds. *Educational Leadership*, 69(2), 36–41.

City, E.A., Elmore, R.F., Fiarman, S.E., & Teitel, L. (2009). *Instructional rounds in education: A network approach to improving teaching and learning.* Cambridge, MA: Harvard Education Press.

de Luise, V.P. (2014). Teachable moments, learnable moments: Medical rounds as a paradigm for education. *Mind, Brain, and Education*, 8(1), 3–5. doi: 10.1111/mbe.12038

Epstein, J.L., Sanders, M.G., Simon, B.S., Salinas, K.C., Jansorn, N.R., & Van Voorhis, F.L. (2002). *School, family, and community partnerships: Your handbook for action.* Thousand Oaks, CA: Corwin Press.

Every Student Succeeds Act, Public Law 114–95, December 10, 2015; 129 Stat. 1802 (2015).

Ferlazzo, L. (2011). Involvement or engagement? *Educational Leadership*, 68(8), 10–14.

Fullan, M. (2014). *The principal: Three keys to maximizing impact.* San Francisco: Jossey-Bass.

Hargreaves, A., & Fullan, M. (2012). *Professional capital: Transforming teaching in every school.* New York: Teachers College Press.

Joyce, B., & Showers, B. (2002). *Student achievement through staff development* (3rd ed.). Alexandria, VA: ASCD.

Knight, J. (2011). What good coaches do. *Educational Leadership*, 69(2), 18–22.

Leana, C.R. (2011). The missing link in school reform. *Stanford Social Innovation Review*, 30–35. Retrieved from https://www2.ed.gov/programs/slcp/2011progdirmtg/mislinkinrfm.pdf

Marzano, R.J. (2011). The art & science of teaching/Making the most of instructional rounds. *Educational Leadership*, 68(5), 80–82.

National PTA. (2017). For families. Retrieved from www.pta.org

Nieto, S. (2011). Critical hope, in spite of it all. In R. Elmore (Ed.), *I Used to Think . . . And now I think . . .* (pp. 127–133). Cambridge, MA: Harvard Education Press.

O'Sullivan, R.H., Chen, Y., & Fish, M.C. (2014). Parental mathematics homework involvement of low-income families with middle school students. *School Community Journal*, 24(2), 165–187. Retrieved from http://www.adi.org/journal/2014fw/OSullivanChenFishFall2014.pdf

School Leaders Network. (2014). Churn: The high cost of principal turnover. Retrieved from https://connectleadsucceed.org/churn_the_high_cost_of_principal_turnover

Tomlinson, C.A., & Imbeau, M.B. (2010). *Leading and managing a differentiated classroom*. Alexandria, VA: ASCD.

STEP 5

Leverage Powerful Pieces to Accelerate Growth

Simple Strategies

- ▓ Use Speaking and Listening Standards
- ▓ Add Vitality through Vocabulary Immersion
- ▓ Leverage Social Studies for Greater Achievement
- ▓ Amplify Content Area Learning with Literacy Strategies
- ▓ Escalate Energy and Hope with Grant Writing

A successful local businessman provided friendly and astute advice about how to move students to greater academic success. During a casual chat, he said with assurance, "Karen, you just need to load the wagon. Keep piling on good stuff, and better results will happen!" Knowing his company was immensely profitable because of his results-driven management style, I wondered . . . What are those additional "good stuff" pieces that students need for deeper learning that translate into college and workforce success? How do school leaders keep the momentum going and best capitalize on the good stuff, especially that which is right at our fingertips within and outside school walls?

WHAT ADDITIONAL PIECES CAN SCHOOL LEADERS LEVERAGE TO ACCELERATE STUDENT GROWTH?

Bold and agile leaders are needed to transform K-12 schools into dynamic learning environments that enable students to meet postsecondary goals. With the challenges ahead, students must go deeper into understanding standards and core content, communicating effectively, thinking critically, and solving problems. School leaders with strong curriculum, instruction, and assessment components have put the right foundations in place. Strong relationships among students, teachers, and families power up students' growth. However, students are progressing along an increasingly complex path, and school leaders must be aggressive in reaching for additional powerful resources to support them. Students do not just need more of the same but more of the right components that are aligned closely with good teaching and learning and that energize the work of students, teachers, families, and school leaders themselves. What are those right choice pieces, both easy-to-access and aligned to good teaching and learning, that will skyrocket students toward higher goals?

Use Speaking and Listening Standards

Speaking and listening is a BIG piece that is often overlooked in the conversation about how to move students closer to their life goals. Students who have multiple opportunities to communicate effectively have tremendous advantages in their academic development. Becoming well-educated in K-12 schools and later in postsecondary education requires students to be active speakers and listeners in gaining new knowledge and skills. Employers most certainly want workers who can contribute meaningful information, build upon what others have said, and analyze the perspectives and reasoning of others.

RESEARCH TIP

Classroom Conversations Build Intelligence

Resnick and Schantz (2015) find that when teachers lead active, engaging classroom dialogue, students build intelligence (pp. 344–346). Students think aloud, pose questions, share reasoning, and own conclusions (p. 344). Other research confirms the importance of classroom talk and its connections to building knowledge, reasoning, and deeper learning (Michaels, O'Connor, & Resnick, 2008, pp. 284–287). Teachers should provide modeling and practice to enable all students to access deliberate classroom talk (2008, p. 295).

Speaking and Listening Standards

Developing speaking and listening skills begins in dialogue-rich classrooms. Principals and teachers should leverage the Common Core State Standards (CCSS) for Speaking and Listening to intensify classroom instruction (NGA Center & CCSSO, 2010, pp. 48–50). The standards are a best kept secret with their evidence-based foundation and developmental continuum of speaking and listening skills. Throughout K-12, the grade level standards build with specificity. The College and Career Readiness (CCR) Anchor Standards for Speaking and Listening outline postsecondary expectations.

CCR Anchor Standards for Speaking and Listening

Comprehension and Collaboration

1 Prepare for and participate effectively in a range of conversations and collaborations with diverse partners, building on others' ideas and expressing their own clearly and persuasively.

2 Integrate and evaluate information presented in diverse media and formats, including visually, quantitatively, and orally.

3 Evaluate a speaker's point of view, reasoning, and use of evidence and rhetoric.

Presentation of Knowledge and Ideas

4   Present information, findings, and supporting evidence such that listeners can follow the line of reasoning and the organization, development, and style are appropriate to task, purpose, and audience.

5   Make strategic use of digital media and visual displays of data to express information and enhance understanding of presentations.

6   Adapt speech to a variety of contexts and communicative tasks, demonstrating command of formal English when indicated or appropriate.

The first three standards focus on those skills and abilities that students need to engage in purposeful conversations and collaborations, and the next three standards emphasize how students need to present knowledge and ideas in strategic ways (NGA Center & CCSSO, 2010). From this concrete outline of the higher levels of speaking and listening skills that students need, teachers can then decide how best to integrate them into daily lessons.

School leaders should see students applying speaking and listening knowledge and skills across subject areas.

Applications of CCSS Speaking and Listening Standards

Instead of coming to class prepared to summarize the plot of novels, students are ready to consider what might happen next, why certain events are taking place, and what evidence causes further discussion. Students extend concepts and ideas of peers and communicate effectively.

Students engage in critical thinking around artwork. Students examine timelines, paintings, and oral critiques of artists and evaluate the context of the artwork and possible reasons for its development.

After watching a video clip, students assess the speaker's point of view. Did the speaker explain her position logically and concisely? Students ask questions to clarify understanding as well as to call attention to points that are open to further debate.

A student panel shares information and opinions on a topic of interest common to the listening audience. Using proper speaking techniques, students express viewpoints and cite supporting evidence.

Students make documentaries using graphics, video clips, photographs, and sound. Students process data and present information in clear and understandable formats.

Students role play arguments from opposing sides of a question, using appropriate language for their positions and the occasions. Students vary the vocal delivery according to volume, rate, and stress for the purpose of their arguments.

RESEARCH TIP

Classroom Structure Elevates Collaboration and Learning

Students need chances to talk with peers and extend learning. Teachers should structure ways for students to collaborate around the use of language frames, such as sentence starters, that help students build arguments (Frey & Fisher, 2013, p. 82). Scaffolds, such as prompts and cues, should be provided so that all students can engage in conversations at grade level (p. 82). For quality learning, students need opportunities to interact around complex and challenging tasks (p. 84).

Speaking and Listening Study Teams

School leaders have ready forums within the Collaborative Data Protocol to accelerate students' speaking and listening development. Study teams of principals and teachers can begin by assessing students' speaking and listening skills and abilities. What data do teachers now collect that track incremental progress in speaking and learning? Likely, state achievement data do not provide sufficient feedback about speaking and listening progress, so teams will need to rely more on school and classroom data. Within each of the speaking and listening standards, how are students performing?

Is growth evident from year to year among all students, including student subgroups? To show student progress on each of the standards, study teams can create charts and graphs and then write summary statements to help others.

Easy Tips to Build Speaking and Listening Skills

- Include a variety of group formats during classroom lessons to give students opportunities to talk with peers and extend thinking.

- Provide occasions for students to narrate experiences, filled with facts and details, to different audiences.

- Initiate informal conversations with students about controversial topics and encourage students to justify their positions.

- Seek out a robust pool of diverse community speakers who expose students to a healthy exchange of ideas and fresh thinking.

- Design classroom forums where students listen to multiple opinions and challenge ideas in safe settings.

- Set up discussion panels of speakers with differing viewpoints and encourage students to listen closely for reasons and evidence behind their perspectives.

- Pose open-ended questions to encourage students to elaborate with descriptive details.

- Give students more practice in making formal presentations using multimedia components at various school events.

To address gaps in performance and growth, study teams should examine opportunities for students to learn speaking and learning skills. What opportunities do students have for improving their comprehension and collaboration (CCR Standards 1–3)? What opportunities do students have for improving their presentations of knowledge and ideas (CCR Standards 4–6)? Documenting significant speaking and listening activities taking place at all grade levels and within all content areas will point to gaps that need strengthening. For each of the six speaking and listening standards, what and how many major speaking and learning activities exist for students within pacing guides and unit plans? School leaders can use the Major Speaking and Listening Opportunities Chart to map out students' speaking and listening opportunities across grade levels (eResource F).

STORIES FROM EDUCATORS MAKING A DIFFERENCE EACH DAY

While doing car duty outside an elementary school, we watched the first car pull up. The music was blaring loudly . . . thump, thump, thump, the car was even vibrating when it pulled up to the curb. The car door opened, and a student tumbled out. Then, the next car pulled up, and the student lingered at the door while chatting with her father about their diseased ash tree. We overheard the father and daughter plan to monitor the weather until it is dry enough to apply fungicide to the leaves. One student spent his 30 minute drive to school without any opportunities to talk while another student spent her 30 minutes raptly engaged in dialogue about biological preservation. When you take 180 days of conversation opportunities and multiply by 30 minutes to school and 30 minutes from school, you have 180 hours of purposeful conversations per year for the second student. Multiple chances to speak and listen offer students strong foundations for college, work, and life success.

GUIDE TO ACTION

Which students are Academic Ambassadors—that nucleus of 20–25 students who speak well and advocate on behalf of the academic culture of the school? Are these students featured on the school's website, and do they kick off orientation sessions for new students and new teachers to showcase speaking skills? How can school leaders increase their opportunities to demonstrate their speaking abilities and reinforce the school's belief that speaking and listening well do matter?

Add Vitality through Vocabulary Immersion

Vocabulary study is an essential BIG piece that increases academic rigor in student learning. Adding sophisticated words, technical terms, novel phrases, and fresh thinking to all content areas brings new energies to accelerate students in their learning. When the most reluctant students become experts at using new vocabulary words, their confidence explodes, and they lead the charge for more learning.

Vocabulary Connections to K-12 Curriculum

Principals and teachers must be strategic about teaching vocabulary. Principals and teachers will want to look closely at the vocabulary demands within the challenging state academic standards. To illustrate, within the College and Career Readiness (CCR) Anchor Standards for Language, students need to increase their skills in using context clues and in examining word parts (NGA Center & CCSSO, 2010, p. 51). Deciphering figurative language and word relationships are expectations. Students will need to use general academic and domain-specific words and phrases in reading, writing, speaking, and listening (2010, p. 51).

K-12 vocabulary study is not about memorizing lists of esoteric words but instead about focusing on grade level words and phrases that students

---

RESEARCH TIP

School Leaders Must Champion High-Frequency Words

Beck, McKeown, and Kucan (2002) help teachers decide which vocabulary words will be most useful to students. Tier 1 words include basic words that do not require instruction, and Tier 3 words are not as common and most used within specific disciplines (pp. 15–16). Tier 2 words are the high-frequency words that should be the focus of academic instruction; teachers include these words based upon their importance, usefulness, content connections, and deeper learning potential (p. 19).

encounter in rigorous daily instruction. As students read, write, speak, and listen within the higher levels of local curriculum, they encounter challenging words, phrases, and concepts and build their vocabularies. As they read complex informational texts across content areas, students encounter general academic vocabulary words and domain-specific words in context. Literacy-rich classrooms allow students to learn new vocabulary words during daily academic instruction and reinforce relevance and meaning.

Strategies to Boost Vocabulary Growth

School Improvement Focus

With study teams already established within the Collaborative Data Protocol, school leaders are ready to act. Principal and teacher teams should use formative and summative data to assess students' vocabulary development. Likely, state tests, schoolwide assessments, and classroom assessments have language arts standards data that are disaggregated by vocabulary skills and abilities. How are students performing from year to year on the different vocabulary standards? How does student performance on vocabulary standards compare to student performance on the other language arts standards? Are all students, including student subgroups, showing vocabulary growth?

> **RESEARCH TIP**
>
> ## Vocabulary Instruction Amplifies Learning
>
> In their research about high reliability schools, Marzano, Warrick, and Simms (2014) advocate for a comprehensive approach to vocabulary instruction due to its relationship with greater student learning (p. 70). Other researchers add that vocabulary knowledge must be gained not only from context but also from powerful vocabulary instruction (Beck, McKeown, & Kucan, 2002, pp. 1–12). Classroom instruction should be enriched with challenging word use, word play and discovery, and extensive vocabulary resources (2002, p. 128).

Direct Instruction of Vocabulary

Classroom instruction is pivotal in students' vocabulary development. Teachers should build in segments during instructional routines to explicitly teach vocabulary. Early in the routines, teachers can engage students with interactive demonstrations of vivid pictures, video snippets, or other appealing interactive formats that clearly explain unfamiliar vocabulary words. When students have already interacted with the challenging vocabulary words, they will more confidently engage with the words later during guided and independent work.

Throughout instructional routines, teachers should model uses of vocabulary words to enable students to benefit from multiple exposures to the words. Scaffolds are especially helpful for students with less verbally rich backgrounds. When reading aloud, teachers should model their own thinking as they use context clues to determine unknown vocabulary words. Auditory learners will benefit from hearing many examples of the words in context of the lesson, and kinesthetic learners will benefit from teachers who demonstrate and use word play.

STORIES FROM EDUCATORS MAKING A DIFFERENCE EACH DAY

One teacher is a well-known vocabulary legend. When she first explains her vocabulary study procedures, students become more attentive listeners. For students of all ability levels, she assigns general academic and other high-frequency vocabulary words that students need to be knowledgeable citizens, productive employees, and lifelong learners. All students are given individual vocabulary lists known only to them. Throughout the semester, in strategic times during lessons, the teacher asks students to go to the front of the room and play-act words. For instance, a student may act *parsimonious* with a cashier about spending his hard-earned money. A student may pretend to tromp through a *morass* wearing giant boots. Another student exhibits *benevolent* actions in befriending a new student. Miraculously, students learn vocabulary words in preparation for performing in front of peers. Because of the *serendipitous* drama component and extra processing opportunities, students remember the words and phrases and incorporate more sophisticated vocabulary into the lively verbal classroom.

Vocabulary Acquisition during Wide Reading

Students need opportunities to read extensively across all content areas to acquire higher levels of vocabulary knowledge and deepen subject-area understanding at the same time. Teachers should orchestrate chances for students to connect with challenging vocabulary during wide reading. As an example, in science, not all students will self-select a book about DNA replication. However, after the science teacher hooks student interest through a genetic engineering video, she can seamlessly preview wide reading books. To foster persistence for interacting with the genetic engineering vocabulary, the teacher can place definitions and applications of the words and phrases on the classroom website or blog. Exposing students to words, words, and more words associated with genetic engineering will lead to repeated practice with vocabulary and deeper learning of content. And, as students read and accumulate new vocabulary knowledge, they can track their vocabulary acquisition themselves. Watching their own vocabularies expand reaffirms their capabilities as learners.

Schoolwide Vocabulary Applications

School leaders should rally a team effort to increase vocabulary learning. When school leaders urge teachers and staff to add general academic vocabulary words (unobtrusively!) into the school day, remarkable things happen.

Teachers connect a general academic **word of the week** to content learning. Students benefit from repeated teacher modeling of new words across all classrooms. School leaders send word of the week social media blasts to families to extend vocabulary learning at home.

Media specialists feature **history and etymology of general academic words**. The media center is a favorite getaway for students to look more closely at word origins within the context of primary and secondary sources and other reference materials.

Principals initiate intriguing classroom conversations with a schoolwide **quotation of the day**. Principals can recognize students that are nominated by teachers for using quotations effectively and creatively.

Cafeteria workers flood the lunchroom with playful, **unexpected vocabulary use**. Cafeteria workers can dress in costumes and add rhyme and jingles that commit vocabulary words to long-term memory.

Parent organizations sponsor a Grade Level Feud, patterned after Family Feud, or a Word Bingo, where students apply **general academic vocabulary words** during **competitions** to bring intensity to learning.

Counselors weave **college-going vocabulary** into classroom presentations. Having a college and career-focused word wall in the guidance area gives students multiple exposures to college-related words and phrases.

As part of the vocabulary team, coaches incorporate **athletic and sports-related adjectives, nouns, and verbs** into promotional materials about sporting events. Coaches are privy to a wide spectrum of action verbs that can be sprinkled throughout practices.

GUIDE TO ACTION

School leaders need to recognize Academic Vocabulary Stars. As principals do walkthroughs, they hear students using robust vocabulary words. School leaders can note student names and celebrate vocabulary achievement. Perhaps the school's front hallway showcases a Vocabulary Hall of Fame, or a weekly Vocabulary Scholar earns first place in the lunch line.

Leverage Social Studies for Greater Achievement

Social studies instruction is a BIG piece that helps load the wagon! The game has changed drastically, and no longer is social studies pushed to the side in favor of tested English, math, and science subjects. Due to challenging college and career targets, social studies is jettisoning to the top of the teaching and learning priority list.

Social Studies Connections to College and Careers

Building support for social studies instruction entails widening the knowledge base about its significance. School leaders must clearly communicate to students, teachers, and families about the linkages between social studies instruction and the consequential college and career targets.

Challenging State Academic Standards

Students must meet increased literacy expectations on state standards across content areas, including social studies. Social studies disciplines are rich arenas for increasing student growth in reading, writing, speaking, and listening.

Graduation Requirements

Students need high school social studies credits for graduation. As students interact within challenging content in world history, United States history, government, and economics, they think more deeply about worldwide issues.

Advanced Placement (AP) Courses

Students select from a rich array of AP social studies courses to earn credit and/or advanced standing in colleges. Substantive dialogue and document-based writing in AP courses lead to deeper learning.

College Admissions Tests

Passages in history, civics, economics, geography, psychology, and sociology await students on college admissions tests. Specifically, the SAT requires students to apply literacy and math knowledge to social studies contexts and synthesize information and solve problems within social studies content (The College Board, 2017). The SAT also focuses on United States founding documents, global issues, and informed citizenship (2017).

Career and Technical Education

As students participate in social studies research and real-world projects, they develop important work habits that help them navigate career and technical education pathways. Social studies instruction immerses students in critical thinking, problem-solving, and communication activities to help students hone skills that are valued by employers.

RESEARCH TIP

Social Studies Instruction Leads to Deeper Learning

Social studies instruction prepares students for higher levels of college and workplace challenges with its emphasis on critical thinking, problem solving, and collaboration (National Council for the Social Studies, 2016, p. 180). Social studies instruction actively engages students in meaningful, ethical, and interrelated disciplinary learning (pp. 180–182).

Social Studies Active Learning Components

With significant connections to college and career targets, social studies education is a powerful driver for student growth. School leaders must capitalize on the unique and robust aspects of social studies instruction that take place during and outside the school day. Students will benefit from greater access to social studies content and more practice in critical reading, writing, speaking, listening, and thinking.

High-impact components within social studies instruction will strengthen academic skills, improve attitudes, and build better citizens.

Community as a Classroom

To be intelligent and informed citizens, students must experience the world beyond school walls and away from computer screens. School leaders should investigate ways for students to explore aspects of history, geography, economics, civics, sociology, and psychology within their own communities. The local community offers ways for students to make classroom connections with real people, places, and events.

Community events, such as health fairs and music festivals, provide a multitude of openings for students to experience cultural diversity. Community parks offer students real ways to understand the environmental issues that are changing the world. As they seek creative solutions and work through pressing community issues, students improve problem-solving abilities and develop persistence in learning. Local museums feature galleries and exhibitions that help students gain context for classroom learning. Joining museum councils and clubs bolsters student agency and more learning!

GUIDE TO ACTION

Teachers and fourth grade classes can take advantage of the Every Kid in a Park Program (White House, 2017) to access free field trips to national parks, lands, and waters. The program offers curricular resources with lesson objectives and activities. School leaders can communicate to families of fourth graders about ways to obtain a yearly pass and extend social studies learning.

Biography and Autobiography Studies

Students improve achievement as needed on the higher levels of standards as they read and comprehend informational texts, such as biographies and autobiographies. As they read, write, and think about real and imaginary people of interest, students blend literacy learning with meaningful content learning. Leveraging biography and autobiography studies across the school will result in a greater volume of student reading opportunities as well as students' increased exposure to a wider range of texts.

An intentional focus on people within curricular areas deepens students' personal ties to learning. Students connect with people who are images of themselves yet also gain appreciation for achievements of more diverse peoples. Looking closer at others' lives brings fresh perspectives and more tolerant attitudes. Studying traditional heroes, literary giants, music and movie legends, epic characters, political and historical figures, sports icons, and inventors and innovators will grow interest and elevate the quality and quantity of classroom conversations. As students experience vocabulary and language of people within varying cultures and time periods, higher levels of content will become more memorable and accessible.

STORIES FROM EDUCATORS MAKING A DIFFERENCE EACH DAY

I listened intently as a veteran administrator quietly contributed to a leadership discussion about a historical narrative that he enjoyed reading aloud to students. He pulled out a small, paperback book with pencil illustrations and insisted the narrative was an easy read for school leaders with a few minutes to join classrooms. He proceeded to tell the story of Daniel Sparrow, a Native American who moves into a new school and has difficulty making friends (Gostick, 2003). He pointed to pictures in the story and relayed key details and facts about the Native American culture. He read softly the awkward dialogue between two boys from different cultures and paused several times to question aloud Daniel's thoughts. Hmmm . . . I could easily envision the toughest students listening attentively to this school leader as he skillfully wove cultural sensitivity throughout the plot to capture the story's spirit. Through the short narrative, this school leader allowed a boy, an outsider from another culture, to join students' imaginations, and in the process, he promoted a more inclusive and respectful school.

Historical Storytelling

Students' right brains love stories. Augmenting social studies pacing guides, units, and lessons with storytelling intensifies classroom learning. Through firsthand glimpses into people, places, and events, students develop curiosity which inspires more history learning. Students improve listening and higher-order thinking skills when university professors, veterans, museum tour guides, and local history lecturers join classrooms as dynamic storytellers. Seasoned storytellers captivate students with shared experiences that will spawn a wealth of group reflections. To add local flavor, principals, teachers, and family members can also re-tell stories heard growing up, helping to open students' minds to a colorful tapestry of local history. By designing a local History Day competition featuring storytelling and other oral presentations, students bring even more intensity to social studies learning.

Service Learning

Service learning connects classroom learning to the larger community as students engage in activities that benefit others. Students learn firsthand that they are capable of making significant changes. Service learning transforms students of all ages into academic leaders and caring citizens. Community guest speakers open minds to pressing social issues and stimulate creative ideas for projects. Classroom and school service learning projects extend inquiry and problem-solving as peers work collaboratively to complete tasks. Students develop empathy and compassion as they become givers of service to others. Reflection activities help students grow academically, socially, and emotionally as they analyze how their attitudes have been altered by their experiences.

RESEARCH TIP

Service Learning Results in Positive Attitudes, Behaviors, and Achievement

Celio, Durlak, and Dymnicki (2011) find significant benefits of service learning. Service learning improves students' attitudes toward self, school, and learning and also improves civic engagement, social skills, and academic achievement (p. 172). Principals of urban, high-poverty, or majority nonwhite schools also documented "very positive" service learning connections with student attendance, academic achievement, and school engagement (Scales, Roehlkepartain, Neal, Kielsmeier, & Benson, 2006, p. 48).

Citizenship Learning

To be successful in college, careers, and life, students need to know how to act in ways that benefit themselves, their local environments, and the global community. Citizenship learning powers up social studies learning with active learning and civic engagement. How can principals and teachers best prepare students to be leaders and active participants in our democracy? Social studies classrooms will give students chances for active democracy learning through a wide variety of performance projects and rich guest speaker forums. As an example, school leaders can invite political action groups, such as the League of Women Voters, to educate students about voting responsibilities and about evaluating candidate viewpoints critically.

RESEARCH TIP

Global Ready Students Need the "Four Cs"

The National Education Association (NEA) interviewed leaders from multiple organizations to determine which twenty-first century skills were most needed in preparing K-12 students for citizenship and the global economy. Research was conclusive that, along with subject matter knowledge, students need to develop the "Four Cs" of critical thinking, communication, collaboration, and creativity (2012, p. 5). Content learning is strengthened when the "Four Cs" are integrated into classroom learning (2012, p. 30).

School leaders should leverage local opportunities for citizenship learning to accelerate communication, collaboration, and critical thinking skills. Attending a city council meeting enables students to see specific ways that they can contribute to civic and political action. Speaking and listening to the sheriff at the local jail helps students comprehend the need for rules and laws in a democratic society. Participation in mock trials at the juvenile center engages students in critical thinking and reasoning skills.

Interviewing the Mayor and other government officials gives students a better understanding of decision-making processes. Participating in a model congress in a local courtroom allows students to understand policy development and the need for action.

As students watch governmental and other local groups engage within real problems, they will learn how local leaders respect the rights and interests of others. Exposure to real situations helps students become more open-minded and tolerant. Current events discussions will become richer and more relevant when students are passionate about controversial issues that impact people they know. Through consistent reinforcement of civics concepts in classrooms and active community engagement, students will become better scholars and local and global citizens.

Amplify Content Area Learning with Literacy Strategies

Another BIG piece in propelling students forward in learning includes every subject BUT English/language arts. When school literacy scores are published, many people automatically think English/language arts classes solely determine the results. As important as this core subject is to student achievement, other content areas are deal breakers in whether students fully develop literacy skills. School leaders must guide the way for all teachers to make powerful contributions to accelerate students' literacy development.

To be college and career ready, students must be able to read complex informational text within a variety of disciplines with less support than they received in K-12 (NGA Center & CCSSO, 2010, p. 4). Across science, history/social studies, and technical disciplines, students must gain strong general and discipline-specific knowledge and skills through reading, writing, speaking, and listening (p. 7). Likewise, the SAT features passages, including words, phrases, and graphics, from different disciplines, and requires students to apply knowledge to respond to questions, make meaning, and solve problems within the science and social studies disciplines (The College Board, 2017).

RESEARCH TIP

Disciplinary Literacy Incites Connections and More Learning

C. Shanahan and T. Shanahan (2015) share that students headed for college must be proficient at reading in the disciplines (p. 13). Disciplinary literacy helps students gain knowledge and skills as if they are specialists inside the discipline, actively thinking, analyzing, and discovering content (p. 12). Disciplinary literacy encourages students to read, think, and solve problems as a part of those disciplines, making important connections and developing more abilities (2014, p. 629).

Discipline-specific Literacy Instruction

Students need general literacy strategies, like previewing texts, taking notes, and summarizing, that can be applied across all disciplines to improve reading comprehension. General literacy strategies help students better anticipate, monitor, and reflect upon their learning. However, along with these more general strategies, students need to be supported with literacy instruction that is more discipline-specific.

Having shared beliefs about the need for deeper learning in all subject areas builds motivation to strengthen disciplinary literacy. Principals and teachers will want to collaborate around the *why* and the *how* of disciplinary literacy in school improvement work. School leaders can jigsaw articles from research journals, state standards documents, college admission guidelines, and employment materials that highlight the need for more rigorous reading, writing, and thinking within specific content areas.

The Reading Standards for Literacy in History/Social Studies 6–12 and the Writing Standards for Literacy in History/Social Studies 6–12 (NGA Center & CCSSO, 2010, pp. 61–65) can be leveraged as evidence-based springboards for improving literacy instruction. Simply collaborating around important terms within the standards paves the way for designing more powerful instruction. Principals and teachers can design performance tasks

RESEARCH TIP

Literacy and Discipline-Specific Teachers Should Collaborate

Fang and Coatoam (2013) emphasize that students benefit from instruction in both general and discipline-specific literacy strategies (p. 630). Literacy teachers and discipline specific teachers should collaborate around content, ways of thinking, and performance tasks specific to the disciplines (p. 630). C. Shanahan and T. Shanahan (2014) emphasize the potential of professional learning around disciplinary literacy (p. 629). The top literacy programs include literacy and disciplinary teachers working together to engage students (p. 631).

within units and lessons using the higher levels of language within the CCSS to enhance rigor and engagement within classrooms.

Examples of Performance Tasks that Activate Literacy in the Disciplines

Analyze multiple print and digital sources—In *history classes,* students cross-reference evidence from multiple primary and secondary sources and produce their own accounts of historical events.

Integrate key terms and domain-specific words and phrases—In *career and technical education classes,* students highlight key terms and specialized words within safety manuals. Students converse and use the specialized words and phrases in performing various operations.

Discuss how key ideas and events contribute to a central idea—In *government classes,* students trace the development of political figures throughout their lifetimes, noting how changes in speeches and written correspondence contribute to stances on controversial issues.

Assess the author/artist's point of view or purpose—In *art classes,* students grapple with biographical accounts and paintings of the same artist and corroborate reasons behind the big ideas within the artist's works.

Identify main procedures or steps when performing tasks—In *math classes,* students design flow charts with accompanying explanations to clarify the reasoning behind solving problems.

Study texts and visual information together—In *science classes,* students examine procedural texts alongside figures, graphs, and timelines and discover relationships among concepts. Students work together to review evidence and process data to enhance understanding.

Talk about facts and opinions within texts and other research—In *health classes,* students examine research and watch advertisements about the same topic. Students analyze vocabulary and technical terms used by clinicians and compare that to language used by advertisers to better comprehend facts and opinions.

STORIES FROM EDUCATORS MAKING A DIFFERENCE EACH DAY

Every school leader knows the anxiety that accompanies the news of an unsupervised classroom. Graduate courses do not prepare leaders for this! One Friday afternoon when the school was low on substitute teachers, multiple classes had to be combined. Students were quickly escorted into the study hall and told to take out something to read. After loud groans, students pulled out digital devices and books. For those of us monitoring, it was fascinating to see which disciplines most engaged students. Health and wellness was number one with students taking surveys about refusal skills, planning vegetarian diets, drawing diagrams of genetic histories, writing notes about time management, and charting personal health behaviors. By their own election, students were reading, writing, and thinking about health and wellness content. School leaders must not overlook chances to boost literacy development in subject areas like health and wellness that have possibilities to delight and inspire students.

Disciplinary Literacy and Professional Development

School leaders should focus professional learning around disciplinary literacy in ways that make sense for their schools. Like students, principals and teachers can become detectives themselves as they investigate ways to accelerate literacy and generate deeper learning within the disciplines (Shanahan & Shanahan, 2014). Experimenting with different professional development formats, such as learning centers, can be informative, collaborative, and enjoyable at the same time. Possible learning tasks for the centers are endless as school leaders contemplate: How can teachers accelerate opportunities for students to engage in disciplinary literacy in more meaningful ways?

Professional Learning Centers about Disciplinary Literacy

Center 1: Without a focused agenda, teachers need chances to simply spend time talking about literacy expectations outside English/language arts classes. The Reading Standards for Literacy in History/Social Studies 6–12 and the Writing Standards for Literacy in History/Social Studies 6–12 are ready sources to anchor the discussion (NGA Center & CCSSO, 2010, pp. 61–65). Teachers should reflect on the standards' requirements for students to pay attention to ideas and details, to analyze structures within texts, to research evidence from multiple sources, and to evaluate arguments.

Center 2: Teachers can play with the concept of evidence within the standards. What kinds of evidence will students find across all content areas? Teachers should focus on what it means to look for evidence from the point of view of professionals in those areas. What does it mean to learn like a biologist? When teachers hear from colleagues about how students are seeking evidence in other areas, they will generate more ideas to try in their own classrooms.

Center 3: Teachers can simply explore the opportunities that students have to interact with different, substantive content in the various disciplines. What curricular opportunities do students have now that enable then to apply their literacy skills? Pulling passages from texts within various subjects and having conversations around the intellectual challenges demanded of students will build awareness of more literacy opportunities. How can teachers further strengthen students' literacy development in the different disciplines with supplemental materials?

Center 4: Looking at elaborate visuals in different disciplines will be interesting. In technical works, students need to follow specific procedures that include specialized words, symbols, and diagrams. In science, students interpret data within graphs and figures. What strategies in each of the specific disciplines will students find most useful to communicate information and illustrate concepts?

Center 5: Teachers can collaborate around the big ideas that students are learning across all content areas. How can teachers create cross-curricular instructional activities that use reading, writing, speaking, and listening to solidify understanding of the big ideas? How are the big ideas communicated across the school? How can teachers more regularly strengthen connections among big ideas to push students to deeper learning?

Escalate Energy and Hope with Grant Writing

Grant writing is the BIG piece that catapults teaching and learning way beyond that next level. School leaders must be right there at the intersection of evidence, best teaching practices, high energy, and creativity—ready to go after those right opportunities that bring students closer to postsecondary and workplace success. Grants are transformative, ushering in positive changes that may not have been possible without the grant focus and resources. Grants that are carefully aligned with school improvement work are powerful assets to fast-track student achievement and growth.

RESEARCH TIP

School Leaders Move Learning Forward

Fullan (2010) highlights "motion leadership" to help principals and teachers propel individuals, schools, and systems forward in simple yet powerful ways (pp. 2–3). School leaders should bring together peers in intentional ways to cause forward movement (2010, pp. 35–36). Doing a few practices well and consistently multiplies outcomes (2010, pp. 54–55).

Grant Outreach and Resources

Too many times school leaders wait for that perfect grant to arrive in the inbox. Perhaps years ago this might have happened, but not today. Due to the economic landscape, grants are more purpose-specific and competitive. Principals and teachers must continuously assess needs, think proactively, and aggressively seek out opportunities.

School leaders should regularly monitor the websites of local, state, and federal groups that offer K-12 grants. Local community foundations are excellent places to begin because they, too, have a stake in improving nearby schools and in bringing community partners together. For instance, community foundations may offer grants to multiple organizations, including schools, that provide literacy programming for low income families. Education foundations may have more targeted grants to support the goals of classrooms and schools. Other grant sources are local colleges and universities who are looking for K-12 partners for larger-scale initiatives.

Examples of Local Groups Who Sponsor Grants

Crime Prevention Programs	Parent Booster Groups
Family and Charitable Trusts	Sororities and Fraternities
Health Education Groups	Symphony and Arts
Hospitals and Foundations	Commissions
Humanities Councils	Youth Institute Groups
Literacy Organizations	Veterans Groups
Men's Service Clubs	Women's League and
Mental Health Boards	Department Clubs

State departments of education are ready sources of grant possibilities for schools and districts. State grants provide programming in specific areas, such as pre-school, early intervention, extended day learning, career and technical education, instructional technology, college and career readiness, and special education. State grants are more likely to have enrollment, poverty, or grade level eligibility requirements. The federal government offers larger grants to local education agencies or networks of schools for established purposes, such as literacy, innovation, special education, counseling, and at-risk prevention (U.S. Department of Education, 2017). Federal grant applications require collaboration of multiple partners and often result in consecutive years of significant funding.

Professional groups, such as teacher and principal organizations, also sponsor grants for classroom and schoolwide projects. Community not-for-profit groups may have smaller grants that align with their missions. Financial corporations, legal firms, large supermarkets, insurance agencies, and other businesses may offer funding for targeted projects. Sports foundations and youth recreational groups may offer grant opportunities around promotional events. Online researching is the best way to access these opportunities. School leaders can simply use search engines to periodically check out local, state, and national grant applications to determine possible matches between grant requirements and school needs.

Grant Writing Process

The worst way for school leaders to write grants is alone in offices or classrooms with the doors shut. Grants are all about solidifying purposes, leading collaboration, and generating forward movement together. With grant work, school leaders can distribute leadership responsibilities and accomplish positive changes simultaneously. Just bringing teachers, students, families, and community groups together to assess potential grant opportunities is energizing in itself. Sometimes individuals from diverse backgrounds need access points into schools, and grant collaboration provides structured ways to make positive relationships happen. Grant initiatives enable stakeholders to join with different partners where they get to know each other well as they interact around common interests.

Figure 5.1 illustrates steps of the grant application process.

Most grant proposals begin with a needs section. Writing that section as a school team fosters a common bond as team members discover student developmental gaps together. School leaders will want to share multiple data pieces from the Collaborative Data Protocol and lead open discussions about aspects of the school and student learning that need strengthening. Examining data together sets the stage for formulating achievable goals with clear and expected outcomes.

Sample Grant Application Steps

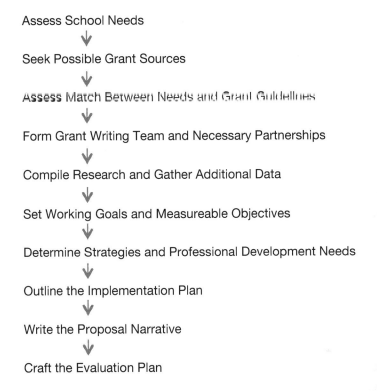

Assess School Needs
↓
Seek Possible Grant Sources
↓
Assess Match Between Needs and Grant Guidelines
↓
Form Grant Writing Team and Necessary Partnerships
↓
Compile Research and Gather Additional Data
↓
Set Working Goals and Measureable Objectives
↓
Determine Strategies and Professional Development Needs
↓
Outline the Implementation Plan
↓
Write the Proposal Narrative
↓
Craft the Evaluation Plan

Figure 5.1 Sample Grant Application Steps

GUIDE TO ACTION

School leaders must be on alert for emails from marketers with ready-made grant proposals. For-profit grant writers are often seeking funding for predesignated programs (and a salary for themselves). Obviously, collaboration of need and consensus about program goals at your school have not occurred. No school leader should feel remorse in quickly deleting the emails.

As principals and teachers work on grant proposals with school and student needs and ambitious goals clearly out in front, adversity will begin to spur on the team members. As the group compiles research and gathers additional data, they become energized with new knowledge and possibilities. The mentality of "us versus others" applying for the same grant incites competition. The grant team begins to coalesce around goals and objectives as they consider more and better support for students.

The team should thoroughly examine evidence-based strategies and needed training as they outline the implementation plan. School leaders will want to confirm with colleagues in the field about the usefulness of potential evidence-based strategies. Many times, creating a plan that builds upon already effective components in the school yields far more improvements than "cherry picking" less aligned solutions from the outside. The grant team may find it helpful to create a chart of implementation strategies and activities. Not only will a visual assist team members with organization as they write the narrative, but it will also serve as a tool for widening grant discussions with stakeholders. School leaders and grant teams can use the Grant Implementation Activities Chart to outline strategies and activities, to ensure good communication, to clarify responsibilities, and to make connections to school improvement (eResource G).

Writing an evaluation plan is the crucial final step. Funders want (and deserve) to know how progress toward the goals and objectives will be monitored and documented. School leaders should guide the grant team to employ quantitative and qualitative measures. Higher education partners can be extremely helpful in designing an evaluation plan that cycles useful data back into grant implementation. Although state test scores are usually required by grant funders, adding focus groups and open-ended survey data to the evaluation plan adds human voices to make significant improvements.

STORIES FROM EDUCATORS MAKING A DIFFERENCE EACH DAY

As grant evaluators for a state agency, our task was to read all grant applications holistically and then rank them high to low. A colleague and I were to read the same proposals, compare responses, and seek consensus. With a big cup of coffee, I began to read. Even though all grant applications addressed the required

questions, they varied considerably. I put a few to the side immediately in which responses did not answer the application questions and
appeared to be recycled from another program. In other instances,
implementation strategies did not connect with needs sections. Quite
a few more were obviously written by professional grant writers
without knowledge of specific school settings; it was not clear who
was going to be implementing what, but the pedagogy was polished!
Then, several proposals quickly rose to the top. Because the principals
and teachers writing the applications were the same ones who would
be implementing them, the proposals were cohesive and thoughtful.
The proposals began with real needs and flowed logically with strong
and passionate voices throughout the implementation plans.
Evaluations were crafted to help principals and teachers grow from
their work and make improvements. Not surprisingly, my colleague
had these same proposals at the top of his list, too.

Benefits of Grant Work

Collaborative grant work in a school is always a win-win situation. If the
grant is eventually funded, it is a highly visible display for everyone that
when school team members work hard together, they can succeed. But
perhaps even more importantly, if the grant is not funded, the grant
work still shows evidence of collective, forward movement. Student needs
have been examined in more detail. Communication lines have been
widened as grant team members pondered bold strategies to solve
pressing school and student issues. And, new partners with community
resources have been part of a cohesive group that can be tapped for support
in the future.

Easy Grant Writing Tips

- Begin the grant application process early and plan to finish early. This
  leaves room for unexpected issues.
- Establish a relationship with the contact person on the funder's website.
  The contact is there to help and appreciates being asked questions earlier
  than later in the proposal stages.

- Take the time to read the Request for Proposal very carefully. Some grant teams just begin with the application steps and do not absorb the entire task.

- Research the funding agency that is sponsoring the grant. Know their mission well.

- Look at abstracts of grants previously funded by the agency. What does the agency value in a grant application? Is the needs section or the evaluation plan more critical?

School leaders need to remember that "here and now is all we get." Sometimes, it is easier to just sit back and wait for others to conduct research and try new strategies to solve problems in education. However, adding grants to school improvement work empowers school leaders, grant writing teams, and entire schools to make leaps forward. Working on grants with critical purposes for improving schools and supporting students grows optimism that becomes contagious. School leaders must grab chances to write grants and bring the additional good stuff!

REFLECTION QUESTIONS

Principals and teachers should prioritize speaking and listening in school improvement work. As a professional development activity, principals and teachers can collaborate around the academic language within the CCR Anchor Standards for Speaking and Listening (NGA Center & CCSSO, 2010). How does the language increase in complexity as students move up the grades? How can we adjust classroom instruction to provide the speaking and listening opportunities that students need?

School leaders should initiate conversations about the importance of vocabulary instruction. How does a student's vocabulary use impact his success in school and in life? Principals and teachers can discuss times that they have used words and phrases and felt successful and perhaps even share moments when they lacked these abilities. How do we enhance vocabulary instruction across the school?

Principals and teachers should leverage ways to promote social studies learning across the school. How can social studies instruction be accelerated through community learning, biography and autobiography studies, historical storytelling, service learning, and citizenship learning? How can we help students strengthen academic, social, and emotional skills as they participate in active social studies learning within and outside the school day?

Principals and teachers should consider how they are promoting discipline-specific literacy strategies that students need to be postsecondary and work ready. Do pacing guides, units, and lessons contain the robust opportunities necessary for students to read, write, and think in deeper ways within the disciplines? How are we promoting disciplinary literacy across the school?

School leaders will want to examine the alignment of grant work with continuous school improvement. How can our school more aggressively pursue grants to address identified student needs? Having discussions about grant writing early in the year will ensure that principals and teachers will be poised and ready to join the grant team when opportunity knocks!

LEADERSHIP TAKE-AWAYS

Principals and teachers should partner with families to strengthen students' speaking and listening skills. Showing families video segments of students engaged in productive classroom talk across subject areas will be helpful. When principals and teachers share concrete ways that students are improving speaking and listening skills at school, families can then extend the learning at home.

School leaders and families should look more closely at students' wide reading choices. Talking in-depth about Tier 2 words will help families better understand how reading more complex texts makes their children stronger readers. Then, when their children want to avoid more difficult texts with challenging vocabulary, families are ready cheerleaders who encourage hard work and practice.

School leaders can solicit assistance from local businesses and non-profit groups in developing common service-learning goals. For instance, energy audits allow students to work with business leaders to track present energy use and devise ways to reduce consumption. Students create spreadsheets to track usage and use science and social studies inquiry and investigation skills to vet possible solutions. Student presentations to community audiences will show results of greater academic, social, and emotional growth.

School leaders should focus teacher learning around disciplinary literacy. Principal and teacher study teams can be in-house experts that use data to design activities around disciplinary literacy. What do our formative and summative literacy data tell us about students' progress? How can we use our data to accelerate learning and engage students in deeper learning?

As school leaders and grant team members submit proposals together, some will be selected for funding and some will not. For those not selected, school leaders must be ready to reimagine other possibilities. Perhaps the school cannot implement all goals and strategies in a particular grant without funding, but if the needs were there and if the ideas were worthy, school leaders should keep moving forward. Why not try a few of the innovative ideas with the resources the school does have?

References

Beck, I.L., McKeown, M.G., & Kucan, L. (2002). *Bringing words to life: Robust vocabulary instruction.* New York: The Guilford Press.

Celio, C.I., Durlak, J., & Dymnicki, A. (2011). A meta-analysis of the impact of service-learning on students. *Journal of Experiential Education,* 34(2), 164–181. doi:10.5193/JEE34.2.164

The College Board. (2017). SAT suite of assessments—Key content features. Retrieved from https://collegereadiness.collegeboard.org/about/key-features

Fang, Z., & Coatoam, S. (2013). Disciplinary literacy: What you want to know about it. *Journal of Adolescent & Adult Literacy,* 56(8), 627–632. doi: 10.1002/JAAL.190

Frey, N., & Fisher, D. (2013). *Rigorous reading: 5 access points for comprehending complex texts.* Thousand Oaks, CA: Corwin.

Fullan, M. (2010). *Motion leadership: The skinny on becoming change savvy.* Thousand Oaks, CA: Corwin.

Gostick, A.R. (2003). *Daniel Sparrow: A Christmas story.* Granite Publishing.

Marzano, R.J., Warrick, P., & Simms, J.A., with D. Livingston, P. Livingston, F. Pleis, T. Heflebower, J.K. Hoegh, & S. Magaña. (2014). *A handbook for high reliability schools: The next step in school reform.* Bloomington, IN: Marzano Research Laboratory.

Michaels, S., O'Connor, C., & Resnick, L.B. (2008). Deliberative discourse idealized and realized: Accountable talk in the classroom and in civic life. *Studies in Philosophy and Education,* 27, 283–297. doi: 10.1007/s11217-007-9071-1

National Council for the Social Studies. (2016). A vision of powerful teaching and learning in the social studies. *Social Education, 80*(3), 180–182. Retrieved from http://www.socialstudies.org/publications/socialeducation/may-june2016/vision-of-powerful-teaching-and-learning-in-social-studies

National Education Association. (2012). *Preparing 21st century students for a global society: An educator's guide to the "Four Cs."* Washington, DC: Author.

National Governors Association Center for Best Practices & Council of Chief State School Officers. (2010). Common core state standards for English language arts & literacy in history/social studies, science, and technical subjects. Washington, DC: Authors. Retrieved from http://www.corestandards.org/ela-literacy

Resnick, L.B., & Schantz, F. (2015). Re-thinking intelligence: Schools that build the mind. *European Journal of Education, 50*(3), 340–349. doi: 10.1111/ejed.12139

Scales, P.C., Roehlkepartain, E.C., Neal, M., Kielsmeier, J.C., & Benson, P.L. (2006). Reducing academic achievement gaps: The role of community service and service-learning. *Journal of Experiential Education, 29*(1), 38–60. Retrieved from http://eds.b.ebscohost.com.ezproxy.indstate.edu/eds/pdfviewer/pdfviewer?sid=514ccdec-90c9–4e1b-a868–3a3d09aeb134%40sessionmgr105&vid=1&hid=120

Shanahan, T., & Shanahan, C.R. (2015). Disciplinary literacy comes to middle school. *Voices from the Middle, 22*(3), 10–13. Retrieved from http://eds.a.ebscohost.com.ezproxy.indstate.edu/eds/pdfviewer/pdfviewer?sid=50273df0-ea5f-410a-8f5e-34ae10dbb267%40sessionmgr4009&vid=2&hid=4202

Shanahan, C., & Shanahan, T. (2014). The implications of disciplinary literacy. *Journal of Adolescent & Adult Literacy, 57*(8), 628–631. doi:10.1002/jaal.297

U.S. Department of Education. (2017). Funding. Retrieved from http://www2.ed.gov/programs/find/elig/index.html

The White House. (2017). Every Kid in a Park Program. Retrieved from https://everykidinapark.gov/get-your-pass/educator

Energize Staff and Students for the Next School Year

Simple Strategies

■ Invest in Your Own Learning
■ Network and Inspire Other School Leaders
■ Induct New Teachers into a Collaborative Culture
■ Nurture (and Keep!) the Best Classroom Teachers
■ Boost Student Growth with Smooth Transitions

The school year has just ended. Students and staff have left for break, yet school leaders remain. Worries persist about wrapping up responsibilities while the upcoming school year looms ahead. Glancing at deserted offices and classrooms is somewhat like peering into a hazy casino . . . lights are blinking, signs are flashing, and people are moving at random. (Of course, a casino environment is intentionally designed this way as profits are at stake.) The good news is that, likewise, school leaders have student achievement and growth at stake, and, they, too, must shape the school environment for success well in advance. Professional learning and innovative planning during the break will result in more purposeful student transition components. When the school year begins, school leaders will be ready and re-energized to roll out teaching and learning activities that cause all students to thrive.

ESSENTIAL QUESTION

HOW CAN SCHOOL LEADERS USE THE SUMMER BREAK TO DESIGN POWERFUL ACTIVITIES THAT JUMP-START LEARNING FOR THE UPCOMING SCHOOL YEAR?

School leaders, amid their other responsibilities, are Chief Planning Officers. How impressive the title sounds . . . to be the ones who look ahead, decide where to direct attention, and lead others in continual growth and improvement. And, what better time for Chief Planning Officers to strategize about greater learning than during the long-awaited summer break!

When summer break begins, though, the planning does not naturally happen. Reality sets in, and low-priority chores that have accumulated all year are still there. School leaders are tempted to walk into the building each day, pour a cup of coffee, and begin to attack piecemeal tasks. It is a certainty that the minutia will be there.

To bring about greater learning for others, school leaders must first prioritize their own professional growth. School leaders must protect their own planning and growing time. School leaders must develop their own essential core of scholarship about good teaching and learning that they can trust when making decisions.

Invest in Your Own Learning

Follow Educational Researchers and Expert Practitioners

Good teaching and learning includes quality curriculum, instruction, and assessment practices in all classrooms and schools. Good teaching and learning focuses on student development of academic and social and emotional skills. Good teaching and learning rests on the belief that all children need chances to grow and learn. Good teaching and learning motivates and engages students. Good teaching and learning involves leaders who build student and adult capacities to keep learning. Good teaching and learning requires forward-thinkers who understand societal and global trends that impact students' lives.

Fortunately, prominent researchers and practitioners provide evidence-based advice about good teaching and learning fundamentals. School leaders should seek out the works of renowned and trusted advisors.

For Recognizing Effort and Persistence . . .
Carol Dweck

School leaders who are responsible for pushing students toward college, career, and life goals need to understand student development. School leaders need a "go-to" research resource packed with real stories about how students grow intelligence. Dweck's *Mindset: The New Psychology of Success* (2006) will help school leaders clearly convey messages that all students can achieve academic growth. Having growth mindsets as opposed to fixed mindsets promotes risk taking and persistence (2006, p. 9). Higher student achievement is possible with focus, total efforts, and a wealth of strategies (2006, p. 67).

For Building Capacity and Leading Change . . .
Michael Fullan

School leaders need uplifting, capacity-building strategies that lead to greater school effectiveness. Fullan (2014) advocates that instructional improvements happen when principals and teachers work together to help the group improve (p. 73). Fullan provides practitioners with sustainable ways to lead change initiatives that strengthen human and social capital (2014, p. 73). Fullan's *Freedom to Change: Four Strategies to Put Your Inner Drive into Overdrive* (2015) offers specific advice about group purpose, improving feedback, accepting responsibility, and influencing others.

GUIDE TO ACTION

School leaders should capitalize on reflection questions accompanying professional development books to apply new learning to school improvement work. What kinds of connections can teachers make among the big ideas of researchers and practitioners? Having groups jigsaw articles and write Big Ideas on giant light bulb posters around the room adds fun and meaning to learning. How can big ideas drive the right changes in the school's teaching and learning work?

For Designing and Evaluating Professional Learning . . .
Thomas Guskey

School leaders need a solid guide that helps them make intentional connections between adult learning and student achievement. What improvements are needed in student achievement? And, then, what kinds of professional development experiences will help principals and teachers make the improvements? In *Evaluating Professional Development* (2000), Guskey offers practitioner-friendly evaluation tools to assess five levels of learning: (1) participants' reactions, (2) participants' learning, (3) organization support and change; (4) use of new knowledge and skills; and (5) student learning outcomes.

For Understanding Societal and Global Trends . . .
Gary Marx

With *21 Trends for the 21st Century: Out of the Trenches and into the Future* (2014) and his summarized guide (2015), Marx shares succinct and relevant scholarship about outside forces that are shaping education. School leaders must be able to talk intelligently and act responsively about societal and global shifts impacting students and schools. School improvement work does not take place in a vacuum but instead depends on leaders committed to developing future-focused plans. Marx makes school connections with trends such as diversity, technology, jobs and careers, ethics, authority, poverty, and work-life balance (2014).

For Curriculum, Instruction, and Assessment . . .
Robert Marzano

Known for his comprehensive research about standards-based curriculum, instruction, and assessment, Marzano gives principals and teachers credibility and confidence to lead school improvement. Marzano's *The Art and Science of Teaching* (2007) provides the cornerstone of good teaching and learning to launch all students toward success. Also, school leaders can monitor progress toward becoming high reliability schools with evidence-based hierarchical levels: (1) Safe and Collaborative Culture;

(2) Effective Teaching in Every Classroom; (3) Guaranteed and Viable Curriculum; (4) Standards-Referenced Reporting; and (5) Competency-Based Education (Marzano, Warrick, & Simms, 2014, p. 4).

For Motivating and Engaging Students . . . Daniel Pink

In order to bring about greater academic, social and emotional, and career development for students, school leaders must understand motivation and engagement. To move others to higher performance, Pink advocates giving choices, providing opportunities to grow, and creating value (2009). How are teachers promoting student development through motivation and engagement? How are teachers using intrinsic rewards across the school? When interviewed, Pink contrasts compliance and autonomy and urges school leaders to create schools that value freedom and emphasize why certain actions matter (Azzam, 2014, pp. 14–15).

For Meeting Academic Needs of All Students . . . Carol Tomlinson

In order to address equity and opportunities for all students to learn, principals and teachers can use Tomlinson's work to adjust content, process, products, and the environment (2014, p. 20). Tomlinson reassures school leaders with the evidence-based *why* and the *how* of providing differentiated learning. School leaders will value her clarity and comprehensiveness for managing groups, scaffolding learning, and designing tiered questions in heterogeneous classrooms. In *Leading and Managing A Differentiated Classroom* (2010), Tomlinson and Imbeau provide specific ways within classroom routines to meet learning needs of all students (pp. 115–135).

Principals and teachers must be able to lead conversations about child development, supervise curriculum, instruction, and assessment tasks, and join school improvement dialogue about scholarship and high-yield strategies. As they interact with students, teachers, and families, school leaders need to be conversant and confident about what works in schools and why. Before principals and teachers can innovate to new levels, they need to make sure that their day-to-day work is grounded in evidence-based practices.

Easy Ways to Spotlight Research and Scholarship

- Use faculty, team, or grade meetings to collaborate around researchers' findings.
- Process research findings in visual formats and display in teacher work areas.
- Select quotations from researchers' texts and webinars to challenge thinking.
- Pique curiosity with trailers about upcoming professional development works.
- Emphasize effect sizes of strategies during school improvement meetings.
- Survey teachers about research preferences and initiate interest groups.
- Use classroom modeling and coaching to apply research lessons.
- Ask teachers to post reflections about applications of evidence-based strategies.
- Have data action teams gather classroom evidence and compare with research findings.
- Invite local university researchers to join school improvement efforts.

Network and Inspire Other School Leaders

With solid research and scholarship in hand, school leaders are ready to seek out practical advice. Accelerating learning for students at the pace expected now demands evidence plus experiences. School leaders need a "boots on the ground" perspective of real time applications and real world results. What are colleagues learning about good teaching and learning applications in classrooms and schools that enable students to make the most gains? How can principals and teachers best capitalize on knowledge from peers and grow as leaders?

RESEARCH TIP

Leadership Development Impacts Student and School Achievement

Louis, Leithwood, Wahlstrom, and Anderson (2010) conclude that only teacher instruction surpasses school leadership among variables contributing to greater student learning (p. 9). Researchers find talented leaders present in all schools showing achievement gains; school leaders set direction and exert influence needed for improved student learning (p. 9).

Principals and teachers must develop their own leadership skills in order to move student learning forward. School leaders have likely thought about reaching out to colleagues outside the school and district to grow learning and build professional bonds. Principals and teachers in neighboring schools are also scurrying to find the best strategies to prepare students for postsecondary and career success. These colleagues would welcome chances to engage with peers in uninterrupted professional reflection and much-needed renewal.

School leaders can develop active networks with colleagues through a range of simple initiatives. It just takes the first school leader to make the networking happen!

■ **Mentoring and Conversation Chats** (Collegial Learning and Support)

■ **Topic and Research Studies** (Evidence-based Dialogue and Observations)

■ **Curriculum Conferences** (Collaboration and Curricular Excellence)

Networking Initiatives for School Leaders

■ **Academic Book Clubs** (Relationship-building and New Ideas)

■ **Data Analysis Circles** (Inquiry and Quality Control)

■ **Project Development Groups** (Initiatives and Wider Opportunities)

Figure 6.1 Networking Initiatives for School Leaders

Easy-to-Implement Networking Initiatives

Mentoring and Conversation Chats

School leaders can initiate fresh associations with 10–20 colleagues in neighboring districts and schools. Chat formats give school leaders informal ways to give and receive attention and support from colleagues. School leaders can structure the chats with brief opening speakers about pressing topics and follow-up with breakout talks. Or, the chat format can consist of table conversations that school leaders can join pending individual interests and needs. Teaching and learning expertise expands quickly, and mentoring easily evolves. Time at the end can be devoted to sharing problems and nurturing a culture of trust. Rotating the chats among schools will expose colleagues to more mentors and more teaching and learning ideas.

STORIES FROM EDUCATORS MAKING A DIFFERENCE EACH DAY

Beginning as a teaching and learning leader can mean moving into a new office with few resources. In one instance I began with a thin manila folder. I was responsible for curriculum, instruction, and assessment for a myriad of students, and that single folder was it. It did not take me long to realize that I was on my own and that I needed help. However, early in my career, that paucity of resources became a tremendous opportunity. I quickly joined a statewide curriculum and instruction networking group and never missed a monthly meeting. I was so grateful to the regional leaders who surveyed us about our needs and created problem-solving forums. One assistant superintendent of curriculum stood out for me as a quality leader with innovative ideas and the passion to make them happen. I took the plunge at one meeting and asked if I could visit her district and learn from her. She not only smiled broadly and said "yes," but she arranged a personal learning session for me. I met with her district's content specialists all morning and then followed up with a late lunch with her to connect and make meaning from my visit. I then had several curriculum contacts for advice, which was most reassuring. I was humbled and grateful for the kindness of this accomplished mentor, and it did not surprise me that she soon went on to become superintendent of an extremely successful district.

Topic and Research Studies

Collegial networking sessions can move to more evidence-based levels. Higher education and K-12 partners can discuss and debate teaching and learning topics, and school leaders quickly become specialists in several areas. Attendees might want to study topics and research related to early childhood education; digital media; science, technology, engineering, and math learning; or English language learners. School leaders from urban, suburban, and rural schools will contribute viewpoints about unique contextual variables and the practicality of multiple solutions. Subsequent visits to neighboring districts then enable school leaders to observe embedded applications of topic and research studies in different settings.

Curriculum Conferences

School leaders should collaborate around curricular excellence to achieve common goals. School leaders in multiple schools and districts adopt materials in the same content areas and benefit from a wider discussion and evaluation of similar curricular programs. For example, school leaders could jointly host a summer Math Curriculum Conference where colleagues analyze math adoption options, looking more closely at alignment with higher standards, program benefits, supplementary materials, technology integration, and professional development. Close-up conversations with colleagues add more expertise and experiences to ensure the best decisions for students.

> **RESEARCH TIP**
>
> ## Leadership Development Includes Mentoring and Networking
>
> Darling-Hammond, LaPointe, Meyerson, Orr, and Cohen (2007) find that school leader development should include study of research and practice and include embedded observation and study, mentoring, and networking supports (p. 146). Principals in the eight state study rated mentoring or coaching and networking as the top two most helpful types of professional development (Darling-Hammond et al., p. 124).

Academic Book Clubs

School leaders can share enthusiasm and glean new teaching and learning ideas in relaxed social settings. To illustrate, school leaders who are curious about character development might choose to read *How Children Succeed: Grit, Curiosity, and the Hidden Power of Character* (Tough, 2012). School leaders can grapple with which academic and noncognitive factors are most needed for student success. Why do some students develop self-control and willpower and others do not? New authors from publishing companies may be interested in facilitating discussions. Online forums eliminate time barriers for busy school leaders, allowing them more flexibility to reflect and respond.

Data Analysis Circles

School leaders can expand their knowledge about using data in more efficient ways to heighten school improvement efforts. Which analytic tools are most useful in which contexts? Experienced and passionate data users are invaluable in making critical linkages among root causes and program opportunities. To illustrate, instead of talking about underachievers with a broad-brush approach, colleagues can focus on the attendance and discipline root causes that impact academic performance. Candid, open dialogue about achievement gap data brings resolution to teaching and learning problems.

Project Development Groups

School leaders can seek out a wider network of colleagues in pursuit of larger-scale initiatives. Sizable successful endeavors result from multiple and diverse connections that spark more possibilities. As an example, leaders from several schools could forge a regional partnership that offers students more internship experiences. How can the larger group design a more varied base of career offerings? Communicating the networking purpose well in advance will draw the right collaborators.

Professional networking enables school leaders to learn much from each other as they expand their circles of expertise. Even though what works in one school doesn't always work in another, healthy discussions ensue about the mix of variables that do make the difference. Networking with colleagues results in collegial bonds, greater collective intelligence, and new energies to spur on good teaching and learning work.

GUIDE TO ACTION

School leaders should schedule a quick lunch with a retired colleague who was a successful teaching and learning leader. Retired school leaders have the advantage of looking back and contributing invaluable wisdom about steering the course of effective leadership. School leaders should tap the expertise and real-life experiences of these valuable mentors.

Induct New Teachers into a Collaborative Culture

One veteran principal was admired by colleagues for her practical, spot-on advice. She would say simply, "Shame on you," to school leaders who would sit back and allow beginning teachers to flounder during the critical early years. I can hear her now: "These are the people you have thoughtfully hired, the people you have welcomed into your school, and the people in which you have already made investments." Colleagues would soak up the words that always made good sense from this veteran principal. She conveyed clearly her belief that school leaders must step up and launch beginning teachers on well-crafted paths toward becoming competent professionals.

Hiring the Right Teachers

School leaders who plan ahead to hire the right beginning teachers reinforce the school's commitment to quality teaching. School leaders can certainly detect a potential teacher's desire and capability to produce student growth. The initial interview should capture the candidate's abilities to adjust to the school's culture of caring and high expectations. By taking the time initially to devise appropriate questions, school leaders ensure a good alignment of candidate qualifications with the school's teaching and learning purpose and goals.

School leaders can use the Teaching and Learning Interview Questions to learn more about candidates' perspectives and abilities regarding student equity, differentiated instruction, family engagement, higher levels of academic expectations, and willingness to learn from others (eResource H).

Comprehensive Teacher Induction Components

During the days and weeks before school begins, school leaders must shift attention to new teachers. New teachers impact full classrooms of students, with the quality of teaching and learning very much at stake. School leaders committed to making sure students are college and career ready will likewise make certain new teachers are 100% teaching and learning ready.

> **RESEARCH TIP**
>
> ## Teachers Need Quality and Systemic Induction
>
> Breaux and Wong (2003) insist that school leaders with ambitious student learning goals must be laser-focused on quality teacher induction (p. 21). Teacher induction improves teacher retention (p. 14). Teacher induction should not be a one-time orientation; instead, the induction should be systematic with active support and continue even beyond the first year (pp. 14–16). Other research confirms the importance of supporting new teachers with professional development (ACT, 2015, p. 2). Research shows that to retain teachers, school leaders should empower them to take on instructional leadership roles (2015, p. 3)

From a purely practical perspective, it makes good sense for school leaders to play active roles in the early careers of teachers. If beginning teachers are given little direction and then struggle in teaching and learning situations, school leaders have to work reactively to solve problems. All of this takes time and worry, and, worst of all, a colleague has been unsuccessful in the process. For the vast majority of new teachers, proactive approaches to ensure their successful development are wise investments.

After hiring the right teachers, school leaders should begin immediately with comprehensive support. Hearing about the school's comprehensive induction plan will nurture early attitudes of professionalism. And, knowing that school leaders care about their professional growth begins a trusting partnership.

Systematic and ongoing teacher induction includes multiple components.

Teaching and Learning Orientation Tours

School leaders should acquaint new teachers with instructional resources. Beginning teachers want to know about textbooks and supplementary materials, media center resources, technology availability, professional libraries, and general supplies. Helping new teachers locate and navigate pacing guides, state standards, unit and lesson plans, and digital resources will help them establish effective classrooms. Veteran teachers are well positioned to lead tours and reinforce good classroom practices. School leaders can ask clubs and teams to facilitate fun activities, such as scavenger hunts, to familiarize new teachers with student programs.

RESEARCH TIP

Induction Impacts Retention, Teacher Growth, and Student Achievement

Induction programs have positive benefits for new teacher retention, teachers' classroom performance, and student achievement scores (Ingersoll & Strong, 2011, p. 225). Math and science teachers, especially, who may have had less pedagogy training, need strong support to keep them in classrooms (Ingersoll, Merrill, & May, 2012, pp. 32–34). Comprehensive induction programs offer more support and are better than induction programs of lesser intensity and duration (Ingersoll & Strong, 2011, p. 228).

Paired Mentoring

Pairing new teachers with veterans who teach in the same content areas or grade levels provides those first credible contacts for content expertise and classroom management. However, just making mentor and mentee coaching assignments is not enough; school leaders must add ongoing support. As examples, school leaders can provide pairs with regular opportunities to observe and analyze teaching practices. School leaders should also structure regular opportunities for the pairs to come together as a larger group. Enjoyable activities might include: smoothies and examining student work, lunch and learning about school improvement, and appetizers and exploring extended learning programs. School leaders can ensure the productivity of paired mentoring activities by initiating online discussions or simply giving the pairs suggestions for coaching conversations. Teacher Mentoring Conversation Starters, an inter-active template, will be useful in stimulating teaching and learning dialogue (eResource I).

Cohort Mentoring

With the majority of new teachers hired before school begins, school leaders should schedule a group meeting. New teachers will become part of a professional cohort, adding another layer to comprehensive induction, as they participate in scheduled activities together. When new teachers belong to a solidified group, they will be more likely to engage together in trying new teaching and learning strategies and sharing candid feedback. New teachers will grow professionally and develop a sense of fellowship from group dynamics. Including second and third year teachers in the cohort mentoring produces more supportive peer relationships.

Professional Development Chunks

Both face-to-face and online learning opportunities energize new teachers throughout the year. New teachers will appreciate gaining new knowledge and skills in small chunks as opposed to attending extended conferences that remove them from classrooms. New teachers will value structured after school sessions such as those that help them better understand school improvement work. Seeking continuous feedback from new teachers will assist school leaders in designing the most useful sessions.

GUIDE TO ACTION

School leaders should assist new teachers in connecting with professional organizations. To illustrate, teachers' unions provide helpful beginning teacher resources and contacts. Also, new teachers should be encouraged to join content-focused groups such as the National Council for the Social Studies and the Association for Career and Technical Education.

Classroom Observations

When school leaders ask veteran teachers about their interests in hosting new teachers during classroom lessons, responses are overwhelmingly positive. Veteran teachers are eager to be models and coaches during the induction process. Beginning teachers will welcome chances to see varied instructional routines and accumulate a repertoire of effective strategies. And, observing teachers outside their grade levels and content areas allows new teachers to tap into a wider range of talents within the school.

STORIES FROM EDUCATORS MAKING A DIFFERENCE EACH DAY

Working as a new teacher in a classroom sandwiched between two veterans had advantages. Both ladies were older and wiser and kindly befriended me with Southern hospitality. During our daily lunches, I loved listening to them tell about being so exhausted that they would go home and "take to the bed." Both veterans graciously welcomed me into their classrooms during my planning period. I would grab some coffee, sit in the back of their rooms, and absorb the happenings. In the first teacher's classroom, students moved smoothly through well-planned instructional routines. Small group activities were purposeful and meticulously crafted. Her firm voice conveyed high expectations, and full engagement of students resulted in equitable learning opportunities. In the second teacher's classroom, students were more self-regulated learners. Sometimes this teacher would begin with poetry. She would immerse students in the elegance of various time periods as she read aloud with expression. She dressed in costumes and used unusual props. She smiled encouragingly as she posed higher order thinking questions and urged students to extend their ideas in writing. These veterans had different instructional approaches, yet both styles were effective in captivating students to learn. I felt fortunate and humbled to learn from the best. My take-away from the visits was witnessing the absolute joy that these teachers themselves experienced daily. Yes, they wanted to go home and "take to the bed," but after watching the efforts that they expended, I concluded that they most definitely deserved to do so!

Principal Shadowing

Comprehensive mentoring should include shadowing the principal to give new teachers an overall picture of teaching and learning. Just listening to secretaries take morning calls enables beginning teachers to better comprehend why students miss school and why students need chances to make up work. And, hearing from a broader constituency, such as a patron's concerns about workforce skills, allows beginning teachers to connect learning in their classrooms to the larger community. And, a cost is not involved. New teachers can come before or after school to observe the principal interacting with students, staff, and families about wide-ranging and relevant issues.

Meetings with Counselors and Families

New teachers will comprehend the significance of individual student achievement when they observe counselors interacting with families. Being informed about higher expectations for students is not the same as witnessing students, counselors, and families designing career plans. New teachers will better adjust to the school's culture of high expectations when they feel strongly connected to families and students' career goals.

Academic Clubs and Games

School leaders will want to quickly assimilate beginning teachers into learning settings beyond classrooms. New teachers will experience satisfaction by interacting with students in extracurricular settings. To illustrate, new teachers can join students in chess matches at lunch or before school. Face-to-face board games build relationships, and even older students find it enjoyable to compete with teachers. Or, new teachers can begin special interest clubs, from gardening to cooking to photography to recycling. New teachers are critical players in bringing about students' academic and social growth.

New Teacher Think Tank

Yes, new teachers benefit tremendously from induction activities designed by colleagues. But, beginning teachers, too, deserve chances to shine for bringing their own skills and abilities to the school. To maximize talents of new teachers, school leaders should challenge the cohort with significant issues and urge them to problem solve from fresh angles. By inviting new teachers to share potential solutions with colleagues, school leaders nurture their strengths and reinforce their abilities to drive a more thoughtful school culture.

Nurture (and Keep!) the Best Classroom Teachers

It's Friday at 5:45 p.m. in an inner city school, the evening before a holiday. Walking through one hallway, a teacher stops right in front of me and states, cheerfully and emphatically, "I love my job." In another hallway two girls are helping their teacher display writing samples on a bulletin board. In a classroom, an algebra teacher and a student teacher are chatting and recording grades. In the conference room, four teachers are laughing together as they re-design the school's data wall. What makes veteran teachers want to collaborate together until well into the evening on a Friday night? What causes this kind of professional satisfaction and commitment to student success? And, most importantly, what do school leaders need to do to retain these best teachers?

RESEARCH TIP

Students with the Best Teachers Make Higher Achievement

School leaders who are committed to moving students closer to college, career, and life goals must nurture and retain the top performers. Research confirms just how critical it is to keep the best teachers. Marzano, Frontier, and Livingston (2011) document the relationship between teacher competence and predicted gains in student achievement (p. 2). Students with highly skilled teachers have greater chances for making higher achievement than students with less skilled teachers (p. 2).

Retention of the Best Teachers

Teachers do matter to student achievement. School leaders must pay close attention to the satisfaction and development of the best teachers. By planning ahead, school leaders can implement thoughtful and effective retention strategies.

Be Present for the Best Teachers

School leaders need to frequently join classrooms of the best teachers. Being present means more than a quick walkthrough; it means spending time in classrooms actively listening and engaging with students. Being present for the best teachers includes recognizing their efforts in preparing lessons and designing activities. Attending family conferences with the best teachers allows school leaders to share in the excitement of students' higher levels of progress. Likewise, being present includes attending academic competitions and extended learning activities that are often sponsored by the best teachers. Being present is a simple strategy that generates amazing results.

RESEARCH TIP

School Leaders Must Retain the Best Teachers

A large research study across urban districts shows troubling retention results for the best teachers (TNTP, 2012). School leaders are not making enough efforts to retain exceptional teachers; in fact, as many as half of the best teachers reported that schools made "little to no effort to retain them" (2012, p. 4). The best teachers felt that schools do not value their skills and do not nurture them within a supportive culture (p. 4). Researchers suggest retention strategies including regular feedback, recognition, leadership opportunities, and more resources (p. 16).

Showcase Skills and Expertise

School leaders need to seize opportunities within the Collaborative Data Protocol for the best teachers to lead. For instance, the best teachers

188

understand the nuances in classroom transitions and can guide classroom action teams in studying instructional routines. The best teachers make expert guides for school improvement rounds. Or, the best teachers could oversee schoolwide displays of quality student work. Families, too, appreciate learning from the best teachers at a variety of "Ask the Experts" forums. The best teachers should be considered first as presenters for school-based professional development.

Empower in Leadership Roles

Too many times school leaders set up committees for important school improvement projects and then leave the committee chair position to chance. Instead, the best teachers need to be tapped early to be the school's instructional leaders. As examples, the best teachers can direct committees in researching and securing quality intervention programs. The best teachers could visit model programs and provide useful feedback to the staff. Of course, the best teachers are ready classroom models and coaches. All staff will notice when school leaders trust the best teachers to contribute in significant ways.

Grow Professional Aspirations

The best teachers add energy and excitement to their profession. School leaders should assist them in helping their voices to be heard and their expertise to be shared. The best teachers can be nominated to serve on community boards and state task forces. The best teachers can also host seminars that include university colleagues about areas of interest, such as, growing intellectual curiosity or building student motivation. Or, the best teachers can set up demonstration classrooms for teachers to visit and engage alongside colleagues. Encouraging the best teachers to share talents via publications, learning communities, or blogs allows colleagues access to their innovative thinking.

Treat the Best Teachers as Special

School leaders should most certainly treat the top tier teachers as special. To illustrate, teachers welcome handwritten notes; sincerity is implied by school leaders personally writing the notes. Also, students talk at lunch and in hallways about creative classroom activities, and school leaders should seek out teachers behind the activities and pay them timely compliments. Even the best teachers need chances to stretch their abilities, and school leaders should help them access varying types of professional development. Locating professional resources and leaving them in mailboxes of the best teachers is always appreciated. And, receiving shout-outs about their outstanding accomplishments during family and community meetings brings broader recognition to the best teachers. The best teachers should always receive a healthy allocation of any additional human resources, such as available parent volunteers, university students, or community interns.

STORIES FROM EDUCATORS MAKING A DIFFERENCE EACH DAY

Creating a culture of teaching excellence begins with school leaders who learn themselves from the best teachers. In my second year as a building leader, a veteran science teacher put a seven page article in my mailbox entitled "What to Look for in an Environmental Science Classroom." She had written a note across the top that I should read the article before conducting her classroom observation. At first I was taken aback because I had just completed leadership classes, and of course, knew what effective practices to look for in all classrooms. But, when I sat down that night and read the article, I realized I had very little knowledge about what to expect in an environmental science classroom. The teacher had shared details and concepts about the laboratory and field investigations that students would be exploring during my visit. The teacher had just filled my backpack with knowledge so that I would be a better observer in a laboratory setting. Knowing more about what I would observe, I felt better entering the room, and was even able to take away relevant points to contribute during the reflection conference. This science teacher certainly improved my awareness of the depth of learning taking place in classrooms of the best teachers.

The best teachers notice when school leaders set a high bar for excellence and hold everyone fairly to the same high standards. The best teachers want to be part of a high achieving and caring culture with leaders who value continual growth and improvement. By openly and thoughtfully promoting their own development, school leaders improve student learning, enhance school culture, and support the best teachers.

GUIDE TO ACTION

School leaders themselves must be members of the best teacher cohort. School leaders create momentum for building quality teaching and learning, and what better way to do this than to be an official member of the group. Reading excerpts at faculty meetings from different content areas and frequently talking about growth in student work shows genuine interest and dedication to teaching. Drinking from a coffee/tea mug that says "I love teaching" says it all.

Boost Student Growth with Smooth Transitions

School leaders should use summer break to make learning sizzle! Students must have opportunities to transition into a new school year filled with hope and armed with strategies to take on higher goals. Principals and teachers, likewise, need opportunities for professional growth and rejuvenation to lead successful, well-rounded learners.

Collaborations That Ready Students for Success

How refreshing for school leaders to engage in uninterrupted creative flow with ambitious colleagues! Principals and teachers should focus on preparation efforts around evidence-based components that intensify student learning. School leaders should look closer at content learning, instructional strategies, personalized learning, and disaggregated data to produce a greater quantity and better quality of academic opportunities for students.

Vertical Alignment of Curriculum

Summer break is the time for school leaders to re-evaluate content learning vertically across subjects and grade levels. The task does not have to involve expensive curriculum modules. Instead, principal and teacher teams need to ask the right questions. How tightly have we linked local curriculum, instruction, and assessments across grades and subjects? As we look across grade levels in the school, in what subjects and at what grade levels do students drop in performance and growth? Where do we see gaps in learning and why? Collaboration around simple questions will assist principals and teachers in readjusting pacing guides and unit and lesson plans to better address student needs.

School Improvement Synergy

Sharing of progress of incoming students between feeder and receiving school improvement teams is a powerful yet underutilized strategy. What goals did the feeder school work toward in their school improvement process? What data show improvement toward those goals? What instructional strategies were most useful for students? How can the receiving school build upon the progress of students coming from the feeder school? What instructional recommendations do feeder school improvement team members have for teachers in the receiving school? How can our combined efforts move students to greater academic levels?

Missed Learning Opportunities

School leaders should dig into discipline reports to uncover ways to gain instructional time for students. Disaggregated discipline data will clarify why students were removed from classrooms and for how long they missed instruction. The number of total hours that students missed learning time may be eye-opening. Yes, students make mistakes and do need to be removed from classrooms. But, what does that look like for all students and student subgroups across the school? Examining root causes of misbehaviors will help principals and teachers better pinpoint gaps in students' academic and social and emotional and academic development. With the luxury of time during break, principals and teachers can rethink ways to tip the scales back to more learning time.

STORIES FROM EDUCATORS MAKING A DIFFERENCE EACH DAY

As a school leader who supervised discipline, I learned quickly that one-on-one student behavior conferences were all about attitudes ... both the student's and mine. In many cases, shifting the conversation from poor behavior choices to future career goals was the game changer. Misbehaving students are sent to school leaders for generous doses of punishment, but somewhere during the lectures, it is critical to change the focus to learning. School leaders must coax each student to look directly at the poor behavior choices, see how they are derailing his goals, and pick strategies to change behaviors. "You want to be an electrician, registered nurse, social worker, or law enforcement officer . . . How are you going to make that happen?" Students who expect another relentless diatribe about misbehavior are instead jolted with compelling questions about future aspirations. What a reversal for students . . . misbehavior seems petty in context with their need for an education. School leaders should talk with students about what matters to their individual learning at every opportunity.

Guidance Placements and Discussions

As part of the Collaborative Data Protocol, action teams collect much formative data. The summer break provides school leaders with chances to look at achievement gaps and devise action plans that open doors for underserved students. With charts and graphs showing inequities in hand, school leaders should lead conversations with counselors and teachers about expanding students' access to enrichment and advanced programs. How can we better communicate to students about the merits of taking challenging courses? How can we promote their confidence to accept the challenges? And, how can school leaders motivate students with potential who do not opt for challenging academic programs? Families will appreciate individual contacts to participate in the discussions.

Community Connections to Academic Excellence

Each year should be a fresh start for students and families in building academic excellence. Over the break, school leaders can work with community businesses and agencies to communicate the importance of academic excellence. Shattering disinterest and disillusionment about education benefits the entire community, but especially families with children who feel disconnected from school. By taking advantage of everyday venues, school leaders can spread know-how about the school's extensive programming opportunities that accelerate students' learning. Community billboards can feature local students in music performances. Families who attend youth sporting events will notice sign-up dates for after school enrichment clubs. Families shopping at local grocery and dollar stores will recognize names and faces of art contest winners. Families will see more and more evidence of academic excellence and discover new hope for their children. Innovative marketing of academic excellence will result in more families seeking out academic programs for their children.

RESEARCH TIP

Student Transitions Improve School Climate

School leaders need to take advantage of every opportunity to improve learning as students move from one school year to the next. In order to improve school culture, Gruenert and Whitaker (2015) advocate leveraging certain points within the school year in which students and staff are most receptive to change. Due to its advantage of following the summer break and additional preparation time, the beginning of the school year is the strongest point to leverage (pp. 135–136).

Student Activities that Amplify Learning

As students enter unfamiliar buildings or the same buildings after extended periods of time, they are anxious about new teachers, new peers, and new academic expectations. School leaders must have solid transition plans in place to fully support all incoming students. Principals and teachers should implement thoughtful strategies that transition students into high achieving and caring cultures.

Positive Growth Mindset Messages

School leaders should welcome new and returning students and families into school environments that exude optimistic growth mindsets. School leaders who weave positive "can-do" words and phrases into speeches, conversations, and actions will ameliorate any defeatist thoughts. In opening meetings, school leaders should build on the growth mindset theme by previewing strategies that will set students up for success. For instance, school leaders can highlight the school's writing center and math help desk that enable students to persevere in rigorous classes. Families will encourage their children to take on challenges when they believe that efforts will determine future outcomes.

RESEARCH TIP

Mentoring Programs Change Attitudes and Learning

School-based mentoring programs show increased academic outcomes in general, including better quality of classroom work, improved quantity of homework, and improved student beliefs about their academic abilities (Jucovy, 2008, p. 5). Cannata, Garringer, MacRae, and Wakeland (2005) provide school-based mentoring resources that promote academic development. Mentoring involves making linkages with available resources, preparing mentors, and focusing on mentees' academic skills (2005, p. 1). Improving academics happens as mentees perceive support, enhance self-esteem and confidence, and change attitudes about learning (2005, p. 13).

Mentoring and Leadership Programs

Making connections among students early in the school year doubles students' chances for success. For the student mentees, they are afforded access to critical resources for success. For the student mentors, unparalleled opportunities abound to coach others during academic and social activities. As an example, academic mentoring can involve study skills strategy sessions. Mentees benefit from instructional support while student mentors reinforce their own positive organizational habits. By interacting together in mentoring activities, all students improve communication and inter-personal skills.

STORIES FROM EDUCATORS MAKING A DIFFERENCE EACH DAY

An inspiring music mix is blaring! Over 300 middle school students are in the gymnasium, half on each side, as the cross country team struts proudly through the center aisle. Other school clubs and groups follow, many in costume and school spirit attire. After the opening pep rally, at-risk elementary students will be paired with middle school students to begin an intensive, two week preparatory boot camp. Mentors and mentees will participate in academic and social activities that give mentees tools for success in the upcoming school year. Instead of waiting for at-risk students to struggle, school leaders are proactive with this school transition advantage. A boot camp intervention quickly accelerates the menu of positive choices for at-risk students. To illustrate, during the camp, all students participate in "speed mentoring" (like speed dating) where they meet quickly with diverse student leaders of sports teams, academic competitions, clubs, and other groups to educate them early about positive activities. And, for student leaders, engaging alongside at-risk students helps push their boundaries to think differently about ways they can serve and learn from others. Both older leaders and at-risk students develop intellectually and emotionally through well-crafted peer connections.

Clubs and Interest Groups

The new school year must be all about joining, joining, and more joining! Clubs allow students to engage in the diverse programming that they may not have access to during the school day. Clubs build on students' interests and abilities and brighten future opportunities. Teacher data action teams can investigate extracurricular data about clubs and interest groups. How many students participate? Why are some students not participating? Are numbers increasing or decreasing over the past several years? How will the school accelerate club and interest group engagement? Being overzealous and pouring too many students into clubs and groups would be a good problem to have.

GUIDE TO ACTION

Chess clubs ignite intellectual and social and emotional development. As students struggle with adversity during chess matches, they build grit and perseverance. Within supportive clubs, students see that practicing sequenced critical thinking and problem solving leads to better capabilities. Healthy competition promotes team building and character development. How can more students access academic clubs like chess that welcome players at all levels?

Schoolwide Academic Competitions

School leaders who drive more involvement in academic competitions link daily classroom learning with after school chances for more applications of knowledge and skills. Groups who sponsor academic bowls often align competition themes with state standards so that students who practice for academic competitions are deepening learning in multiple content areas. Competing on teams teaches students to set goals and work together in more rigorous learning. And, for students who may not make the final school academic team, they still have gained the benefits of practicing important skills and developing resiliency associated with healthy competition.

Easy Ways to Recruit Students for Academic Competitions

- Ask teachers to make personal contacts to invite reluctant students.

- Post student testimonials about the benefits of academic competitions.

- Have students recruit peers with eye-catching post cards and social media.

- Share academic competition study materials at the school's curriculum fair.

- Educate families about the benefits of extracurricular participation.

- Highlight academic teams in posters and pictures around the school.

- Provide exposure to team competitions at as many school functions as possible.

- Ask student mentors to bring their mentees to watch competition activities.

- Host academic competition receptions to honor students and families.

- Find ways to help academic coaches sponsor pizza and practice events.

- Vary practice times to eliminate transportation as a participation barrier.

- Track success of academic competitions and share in many forums.

Agency and Self-Directed Progress

School leaders need to work with feeder schools to allow students to build agency in learning. By compiling student work samples from grade to grade, students will see that completing challenging work and persisting with tasks are valued at the new school. E-portfolios help students and teachers easily organize work products across grades and schools. When students own academic progress, agency becomes embedded in the school culture. School leaders can set up family and teacher meetings early in the year for students to review work and solidify ambitious goals. When teachers create classroom opportunities for students to talk about their prior learning and new goals, they build communities of learners.

Student transition plans are all about setting ambitious goals with high-yield strategies. School leaders can use a visual to make plans transparent and inviting so that teachers, families, and community members can join in and provide support. School leaders can use Transition Goals and Strategies Skyrocket Student Success as an example of how to build awareness and momentum around the school's transition plan (eResource J).

The actions that school leaders take during the school break do matter! Every student needs and deserves a fresh start each year. Reimagining ways to transition students and to engage them throughout the year are smart investments. Principals and teachers who throw aside the minutia and prioritize and prepare for the upcoming school year raise energy levels and inspire higher learning.

REFLECTION QUESTIONS

School leaders need to think about their own efficacy as well as the school's ability to improve student learning. In the upcoming year, how can school leaders improve their own leadership skills and contribute more effectively to the school's high achieving and caring culture? What can we learn from prominent researchers and scholars about good teaching and learning fundamentals to strengthen school improvement work?

School leaders should reflect on ways to extend multi-school networking opportunities to other groups. Mentoring and coffee conversation chats could be extended to teachers and counselors who would benefit from wider discussions. Likewise, teachers and families will value attending curriculum conferences to hear different viewpoints about textbook adoption. Networking with like colleagues in neighboring schools expands reflections about teaching and learning practices that benefit students.

School leaders should reflect regularly upon the effectiveness of their teacher induction process. Quick surveys throughout the year will give timely feedback to adjust current activities. Conducting new teacher focus groups at the end of the school year will provide specific feedback for program improvement. For instance, new teachers can elaborate about ways that professional learning could be better embedded into daily practices.

As a self-reflection activity, school leaders should make a list of all teachers and then estimate with tally marks the contacts they made with teachers over the prior year. Scheduled evaluations and observations in classrooms do not count. Instead, school leaders should think about informal classroom visits, spontaneous hallway and lunch chats, and other personal contacts. How are the tally marks lining up? Has adequate time been spent with the best teachers? It will be interesting to reflect about time spent in classrooms of less effective teachers as compared with time spent with the best teachers. How can school leaders find ways to increase time spent with the best teachers?

School leaders must rethink fresh ways of ensuring early success for all students. How are new students welcomed into the school? Are they linked immediately to student groups with similar interests and aspirations? Are they invited to participate in clubs, interest groups, and academic competitions? Are they signed up by default in the highest levels of classes of which they are capable? How can principals and teachers better connect incoming students to activities that give them more chances for academic growth and pave the way for more life successes?

LEADERSHIP TAKE-AWAYS

School leaders will project credibility and self-confidence from studying the advice of trusted researchers and scholars. Whether they are trying different formative assessments or leading conversations about developing caring citizens, school leaders will have evidence in hand to harness energies around making real improvements. Principals and teachers can then apply these evidence-based teaching and learning foundations to design their own quality school improvement tools.

School leaders can ramp up networking initiatives by including state contacts. Networking with state partners is a productive leadership habit. Many state education departments have consultants who would welcome an invitation to share expertise at a summer forum of school leaders. As examples, state administrators for assessment, textbook adoption, after school programs, and professional development are often available to consult with schools. By including state partners, school leaders forge a multi-dimensional coalition of mentoring support.

School leaders will attend professional development conferences, district meetings, and community events throughout the school year. During the summer break, school leaders should plan ahead and pencil in names of new teachers to invite to these events. New teachers will be honored to attend and learn alongside school leaders, and car rides foster reflective conversations that build knowledge and better relationships.

The best classroom teachers may be willing to help new teachers develop a comprehensive repertoire of instructional strategies. School leaders should encourage the best teachers to create a Schoolwide Strategies Library, a database of teachers modeling evidence-based strategies across all content areas. The searchable database will allow new teachers to watch colleagues demonstrate effective classroom strategies at various grade levels or content areas.

The school's transition activities should excite and motivate both new and returning students. School leaders must educate students and families about the school's cohesive and comprehensive web of support. Communicating the plan's components frequently and widely will make the transition process welcoming, transparent, and easily accessible. Designing a visual together will coalesce knowledge and support around the school's transition components. Investing in students now will ignite their desires and capabilities for learning and translate into a larger, broader, and more diverse pool of student leaders. School leaders who aim higher with powerful transition plans will activate and accelerate students who will aim higher as well.

References

ACT. (2015). *The condition of future educators*. Retrieved from http://www.act.org/content/dam/act/unsecured/documents/Future-Educators-2015.pdf

Association for Career and Technical Education. (2017). www.acteonline.org

Azzam, A.M. (2014). Motivated to learn: A conversation with Daniel Pink. *Educational Leadership, 72*(1), 12–17.

Breaux, A.L., & Wong, H.K. (2003). *New teacher induction: How to train, support, and retain new teachers*. Mountain View, CA: Harry K. Wong Publications.

Cannata, A., Garringer, M., MacRae, P., & Wakeland, D. (2005). Making the grade: A guide to incorporating academic achievement into mentoring programs and relationships. Retrieved from the Education Northwest website: http://educationnorthwest.org/resources/school-based-mentoring-resources

Darling-Hammond, L., LaPointe, M., Meyerson, D., Orr, M.T., & Cohen, C. (2007). Preparing school leaders for a changing world: Lessons from exemplary leadership development programs. Retrieved from the Wallace Foundation website: http://www.wallacefoundation.org/knowledge-center/Documents/Preparing-School-Leaders.pdf

Dweck, C.S. (2006). *Mindset: The new psychology of success.* New York: Ballantine Books.

Fullan, M. (2015). *Freedom to change: Four strategies to put your inner drive into overdrive.* San Francisco: Jossey-Bass.

Fullan, M. (2014). *The principal: Three keys to maximizing impact.* San Francisco: Jossey-Bass.

Gruenert, S., & Whitaker, T. (2015). *School culture rewired: How to define, assess, and transform it.* Alexandria, VA: ASCD.

Guskey, T.R. (2000). *Evaluating professional development.* Thousand Oaks, CA: Corwin Press.

Ingersoll, R., Merrill, L., & May, H. (2012). Retaining teachers: How preparation matters. *Educational Leadership, 69*(8), 30–34.

Ingersoll, R.M., & Strong, M. (2011). The impact of induction and mentoring programs for beginning teachers: A critical review of the research. *Review of Educational Research, 81*(2), 201–233. doi: 10.3102/0034654311403323

Jucovy, L. (2008). The ABCs of school-based mentoring: Effective strategies for providing quality youth mentoring in schools and communities. Retrieved from the Education Northwest website: http://educationnorthwest.org/resources/school-based-mentoring-resources

Louis, K.S., Leithwood, K., Wahlstrom, K.L., & Anderson, S.E. (2010). Investigating the links to improved student learning: Final report of research findings. Retrieved from http://www.wallacefoundation.org/knowledge-center/Documents/Investigating-the-Links-to-Improved-Student-Learning.pdf

Marx, G. (2014). *21 trends for the 21st century: Out of the trenches and into the future.* Bethesda, MD: Education Week Press.

Marx, G. (2015). *A guide to 21 trends for the 21st century: Out of the trenches and into the future.* Bethesda, MD: Education Week Press.

Marzano, R.J. (2007). *The art and science of teaching: A comprehensive framework for effective instruction.* Alexandria, VA: ASCD.

Marzano, R.J., Frontier, T., & Livingston, D. (2011). *Effective supervision: Supporting the art and science of teaching.* Alexandria, VA: ASCD.

Marzano, R.J., Warrick, P., & Simms, J.A., with D. Livingston, P. Livingston, F. Pleis, T. Heflebower, J.K. Hoegh, & S. Magana). (2014). *A handbook for high reliability schools: The next step in school reform.* Bloomington, IN: Marzano Research.

National Council for the Social Studies. (2017). www.socialstudies.org

Pink, D.H. (2009). *Drive: The surprising truth about what motivates us.* New York: Riverhead Books.

The New Teacher Project (TNTP). (2012). *The irreplaceables: Understanding the real retention crisis in America's urban schools.* Retrieved from www.tntp.org/publications

Tomlinson, C.A. (2014). *The differentiated classroom: Responding to the needs of all learners.* 2nd ed. Alexandria, VA: ASCD.

Tomlinson, C.A., & Imbeau, M.B. (2010). *Leading and managing a differentiated classroom.* Alexandria, VA: ASCD.

Tough, P. (2012). *How children succeed: Grit, curiosity, and the hidden power of character.* New York: Houghton Mifflin Harcourt.